CAMBRIDGE LIBRARY COLLECTION

Books of enduring scholarly value

Anthropology

The first use of the word 'anthropology' in English was recorded in 1593, but its modern use to indicate the study and science of humanity became current in the late nineteenth century. At that time a separate discipline had begun to evolve from many component strands (including history, archaeology, linguistics, biology and anatomy), and the study of so-called 'primitive' peoples was given impetus not only by the reports of individual explorers but also by the need of colonial powers to define and classify the unfamiliar populations which they governed. From the ethnographic writings of early explorers to the 1898 Cambridge expedition to the Torres Straits, often regarded as the first truly 'anthropological' field research, these books provide eye-witness information on often vanished peoples and ways of life, as well as evidence for the development of a new scientific discipline.

Maori Religion and Mythology

First published in 1882, Edward Shortland's study is an important account of Maori mythology, religion and concepts of authority. Shortland (1812–93), an English-born physician and ethnographer, first arrived in New Zealand in 1841 to work for the newly formed colonial government. He later served as a government interpreter, Sub-Protector of Aborigines, and Native Secretary during his time in New Zealand and spent much of his career interacting with Maori. This concise book is the result of years of careful research into Maori beliefs and customs, based on narratives and songs dictated to Shortland, or written down for him to translate. It includes a particularly detailed account of Maori cosmogony, lists of Maori vocabulary relating to kinship and to the spirit world, several *karakia* (prayers) and extensive notes on the naming and claiming of land and the Maori understanding of land tenure.

T0345417

Cambridge University Press has long been a pioneer in the reissuing of out-of-print titles from its own backlist, producing digital reprints of books that are still sought after by scholars and students but could not be reprinted economically using traditional technology. The Cambridge Library Collection extends this activity to a wider range of books which are still of importance to researchers and professionals, either for the source material they contain, or as landmarks in the history of their academic discipline.

Drawing from the world-renowned collections in the Cambridge University Library, and guided by the advice of experts in each subject area, Cambridge University Press is using state-of-the-art scanning machines in its own Printing House to capture the content of each book selected for inclusion. The files are processed to give a consistently clear, crisp image, and the books finished to the high quality standard for which the Press is recognised around the world. The latest print-on-demand technology ensures that the books will remain available indefinitely, and that orders for single or multiple copies can quickly be supplied.

The Cambridge Library Collection will bring back to life books of enduring scholarly value (including out-of-copyright works originally issued by other publishers) across a wide range of disciplines in the humanities and social sciences and in science and technology.

Maori Religion and Mythology

*Illustrated by Translations
of Traditions, Karakia, &c.*

EDWARD SHORTLAND

CAMBRIDGE
UNIVERSITY PRESS

CAMBRIDGE UNIVERSITY PRESS

Cambridge, New York, Melbourne, Madrid, Cape Town,
Singapore, São Paolo, Delhi, Tokyo, Mexico City

Published in the United States of America by Cambridge University Press, New York

www.cambridge.org
Information on this title: www.cambridge.org/9781108040624

© in this compilation Cambridge University Press 2012

This edition first published 1882
This digitally printed version 2012

ISBN 978-1-108-04062-4 Paperback

MAORI RELIGION

AND

MYTHOLOGY.

WILLIAM ATKIN, GENERAL PRINTER,
HIGH STREET, AUCKLAND, N.Z.

Maori Religion

and

Mythology.

ILLUSTRATED BY TRANSLATIONS OF TRADITIONS,

KARAKIA, &c.

TO WHICH ARE ADDED

NOTES ON *MAORI* TENURE OF LAND.

BY

EDWARD SHORTLAND, M.A., M.R.C.P.,

LATE NATIVE SECRETARY, NEW ZEALAND,

AUTHOR OF

"TRADITIONS AND SUPERSTITIONS OF THE NEW ZEALANDERS."

LONDON:

LONGMANS, GREEN, AND CO.

1882.

PREFACE.

THE Maori MSS. of which translations are now published were collected by the author many years ago. The persons through whom the MSS. were obtained are now, with one exception, no longer living. They were all of them men of good birth, and competent authorities. One who could write sent me, from time to time, in MS. such information as he himself possessed, or he could obtain from the *tohunga*, or wise men of his family. Chapters iii. and iv. contain selections from information derived from this source.

The others not being sufficiently skilled in writing, it was necessary to take down their information from dictation. In doing this I particularly instructed my informant to tell his tale as if he were relating it to his own people, and to use the same words that he would use if he were recounting similar tales to them when assembled in a sacred house. This they are, or perhaps I should rather say were, in the habit of doing at times of great weather disturbance accompanied with storm of wind and rain, believing an effect to be thereby produced quieting the spirits of the sky.

As the dictation went on I was careful never to ask any question, or otherwise interrupt the thread of the narrative: but wrote as nearly as I could every word, being guided by the sound in writing any new and strange words. When some time had thus passed, I stopt him at some suitable part of his tale: then read over to him what I had written, and made the necessary corrections—taking notes also of the meanings of words which were new to me. Chapters v. and vi. are with some omissions translations of a *Maori* MS. written in this way.

Chapter ii. contains a tradition as to *Maori* Cosmogony more particular in some details than I have ever met with elsewhere. My informant had been educated to become a *tohunga*; but had afterwards become a professing Christian   The narrative took place at night unknown to any of his people, and under promise that I would not read what I wrote to any of his people. When after some years I re-visited New Zealand, I learnt that he had died soon after I left, and that his death was attributed to the anger of the *Atua* of his family due to his having as they expressed it, trampled on the *tapu* by making *noa* or public things sacred—he having himself confessed what he no doubt believed to be the cause of his illness.

In Appendix will be found a list of *Maori* words expressing relationship. It will be observed that where we employ definite words for 'father' and 'brother' the *Maori* use words having a more comprehensive meaning, like our word 'cousin' : hence when either of the words *matua*, &c., are used, to ascertain the actual degree of relationship some additional explanatory words must be added, as would be necessary when we use the general term cousin.

A short vocabulary of *Maori* words unavoidably introduced in the following pages, which require explanation not to be found in any published dictionary, are also printed in the Appendix,—as well as a few selected *karakia* in the original *Maori*, with reference to pages where their translations appear, as a matter of interest to some persons.

AUCKLAND, JANUARY, 1882.

CONTENTS.

ERRATA.

p.   8 for "Pendora"   read "Pandora."

p. 21   „   "Herekeke"   „   "Harakeke."

p. 11   „   "Whananga"   „   "Wananga."

p. 24 „   „   „   „

p. 28 „   "manumea"   „   "Manumea."

p. 90 „   "and"   „   "land."

p. 96 „   "conquerers"   „   "conquerors."

PRIMITIVE RELIGION AND MYTHOLOGY.

———◦———

CHAPTER I.

Νόμιζε σαυτῷ τοὺς γονεῖς ἒιναι Θεούς.

THE religious feeling may be traced to the natural veneration of the child for the parent, joined to an innate belief in the immortality of the soul. What we know of the primitive religion of Aryans and Polynesians points to this source. They both venerated the spirits of deceased ancestors, believing that these spirits took an interest in their living descendants: moreover, they feared them, and were careful to observe the precepts handed down by tradition, as having been delivered by them while alive.

The souls of men deified by death were by the Latins called "Lares" or "Mânes," by the Greeks "Demons" or "Heroes." Their tombs were the temples of these divinities, and bore the inscription "Dîs manibus," "Θεοὶς χθόνιοις;" and before the tomb was an altar for sacrifice. The term used by the Greeks and Romans to signify the worship of the dead is significant. The former used the word "πατριάζειν," the latter "parentare," showing that the prayers were addressed to forefathers. "I prevail over my enemies," says the Brahmin, "by the incantations which my ancestors and my father have handed down to me."*

Similar to this was the common belief of the *Maori* of Polynesia, and still exists. A *Maori* of New Zealand writes thus: "The origin of knowledge of our native customs was from Tiki (the progenitor of the human race). Tiki taught laws to regulate work, slaying, man-eating: from him men first learnt to observe laws for this thing, and for that thing, the rites to be used for the dead, the invocation for the new-born child, for battle in the field, for the assault of fortified places, and other invocations very numerous. Tiki was the first instructor, and from him descended his instructions to our forefathers, and have abided to the present time. For this reason they have power. Thus says the song:—

> *E tama, tapu-nui, tapu-whakaharahara,*
> *He mauri wehewehe na o tupuna,*
> *Na Tiki, na Rangi, na Papa.*
>
> O child, very sacred—very, very sacred,
> Shrine set apart by your ancestors,
> By Tiki, by Rangi, by Papa.

The researches of philologists tend to show that all known languages are derived from one original parent source. The parent language from which the Aryan and Polynesian languages are derived must have been spoken at a very remote time; for no two forms of

---

* La Cité Antique par De Coulange.

language are now more diverse than these two are. In the Polynesian there is but the slightest trace of inflexion of words which is a general character of Aryan languages. The Polynesian language seems to have retained a very primitive form, remaining fixed and stationary; and this is confirmed by the fact that the forms of Polynesian language, whether spoken in the Sandwich Islands or in New Zealand, though their remoteness from each other indicates a very early separation, differ to so small a degree that they may be regarded as only different dialects of the same language. The *Maori* language is essentially conservative, containing no principle in its structure facilitating change. The component parts or roots of words are always apparent.

When we consider the great remoteness of time at which it is possible that a connection between Aryans and Polynesians could have existed, we are carried back to the contemplation of a very primitive condition of the human race. In the Polynesian family we can still discover traces of this primitive condition. We can also observe a similarity between the more antient form of religious belief and mythological tradition of the Aryans and that still existing among Polynesians; for which reason we think it allowable to apply to the interpretation of old Aryan myths the principle we discover to guide us as to the signification of Polynesian Mythology.

It was a favourite opinion with Christian apologists, Eusebius and others, that the Pagan deities represented deified men. Others consider them to signify the powers of external nature personified. For others they are, in many cases, impersonations of human passions and propensities reflected back from the mind of man. A fourth mode of interpretation would treat them as copies distorted and depraved of a primitive system of religion given by God to man.*

The writer does not give any opinion as to which of these theories he would give a preference. If, however, we look at the mythology of Greek and Latin Aryans from the *Maori* point of view the explanation of their myths is simple.

This mythology personified and deified the Powers of Nature, and represented them as the ancestors of all mankind ; so these personified Powers of Nature were worshipped as deified ancestors. There is no authority for any other supposition. With regard to the two latter theories above referred to it may be remarked that fiction is always liable to be interpreted in a manner conformable to the ideas prevailing at any particular time, so that there would be a natural tendency, in modern times, to apply meanings never originally thought of to the interpretation of mythology. Man in early days, ignorant of the causes of natural phenomena, yet having a mind curious to inquire and trace observed effects to some cause, formulated his conceptions on imaginary grounds, which, although now manifestly false and absurd, yet were probably sufficiently credible in the infancy of knowledge.

There is a notable mental condition of the Poly-

* Juventus mundi, p. 203.

nesian to which we desire to direct attention. The *Maori* has a very limited notion of the abstract. All his ideas take naturally a concrete form. This inaptitude to conceive any abstract notions was, it is believed, the early mental condition of man. Hence the Powers of Nature were regarded by him as concrete objects, and were consequently designated as persons. And this opinion is confirmed by the fact that the researches of comparative philologists give proof that all words are, in their origin or roots, expressive of visible and sensuous phenomena,* and consequently that all abstract words are derivable from such roots. The absence, too, of all abstract and metaphysical ideas from Homer has been noticed by Mr Gladstone as very remarkable.

I have seen it stated in print that the New Zealander has no sentiment of gratitude; in proof of which it was mentioned that he has no word in his language to express gratitude. This is true; but the reason is that gratitude is an abstract word, and that *Maori* is deficient in abstract terms. It is an error to infer that he is ignorant of the sentiment of gratitude, or that he is unable to express that sentiment in appropriate and intelligible words.

ARYAN MYTHOLOGY.

The Aryans do not appear to have had any tradition of a Creation. They seem to have conceived of the Powers of Nature very much in the same way as the

---

* Max Müller, "Science of Language." Farrar, "Chapters on Language," p. 6.

Maori did, — namely, that the mysterious power of Generation was the operative cause of all things.

Hesiod in his Theogony relates that the first parent of all was Chaos.

From Chaos sprung Gaia (=Earth), Tartarus, Eros (=Love), Erebus, a dark son, Night, a dark daughter, and lastly, Day.

From Gaia alone sprung Ouranos (=Heaven), Hills, Groves, and Thalassa (=Sea).

From Heaven and Earth sprung Okeanos (=Ocean), Japetus, Kronos (=Saturn), Titans.

Hesiod also relates how Heaven confined his children in the dark caverns of Earth, and how Kronos avenged himself.

In the "Works and Days" Hesiod gives an account of the formation of the first human female out of Earth, from the union of whom, with Epimetheus, son of the Titan Japetus, sprung the human race.

So far Hesiod's account may be derived from Aryan myths. The latter and greater part, however, of Hesiod's Theogony cannot be accepted as a purely Aryan tradition; for colonists from Egypt and Phœnicia had settled in Greece, at an early period, and had brought with them alien mythical fables which were adopted in a modified form, in addition to the antient family religion of worship of ancestors.

Herodotus asserts that Homer and Hesiod made the Theogony of the Greeks; and to a certain extent this may be true, for the bard was then invested with a kind of sacredness, and what he sung was held to be the effect of an inspiration. When he invoked the Muses his invocation was not a mere formal set of words introduced for the sake of ornament, but an act of homage due to the Divinities addressed, whose aid he solicited.*

The traditions prevalent in Bœotia would naturally be strongly imbued with fables of foreign origin; and Hesiod, who was a Bœotian by birth, by collecting these local traditions and presenting them to the public in an attractive form, no doubt contributed, as well as Homer, to establish a national form of religion, made up of old Aryan tradition and what had been imported by Phœnician and Egyptian colonists.

Thus Zeus and the other Olympian deities formed the centre of a national religious system; but at the same time the old Aryan religion of worship of ancestors maintained a paramount influence, and every tribe and every family had its separate form of worship of its own ancestors. The prayer of the son of Achilles, when in the act of sacrificing Polyxena to the manes of his father, is a striking instance of the prevalent belief that the deified spirits of ancestors had power to influence the destinies of the living.

"O son of Peleus, my father, receive from me this libation, appeasing, alluring, the dead. Come now, that you may drink the black pure blood of a virgin, which we give to thee—both I and the army. And be kindly disposed to us, and grant us to loose the sterns

---

* Hom. Il., 2-484. Invocat. to Muses :—
   Tell me now, O Muses, ye who dwell in Olympus;
   For ye are goddesses, and are present, and know all things,
   But we hear only rumour, and know not anything.

of our ships, and the cables fastening to the shore, and all to reach home favoured with a prosperous return from Ilium." *

Euripides would not have put these words into the mouth of the son of Achilles had they not been in accord with the sympathies of an Athenian audience.

Comparing the Greek mythological traditions, such as they have come down to us, with those of the *Maori*, some striking resemblance is to be observed. First, there is the fact that both treat the elements of nature, and abstract notions as persons capable of propagating from each other by generation. In both Light springs out of Darkness. The sons of Heaven and Earth in both accounts conspire against their father for the same reason—that their father had confined them in darkness. And lastly the first human female, in both, is said to have been formed out of earth. The first woman, in the *Maori* Mythology, drags down her offspring to Po (=Night), meaning to death. And the first woman of the Greek Mythology, Pendora, introduces all kinds of afflictions as an heritage for hers.

It is also to be noticed that just as Zeus and the Olympian Gods were national deities for Greeks, so their old mythical deities — Po, Rangi, Papa, Tiki, &c., were invoked alike by the whole *Maori* race, especially in the ceremonies required to free a person from the sacred restrictions comprised under the term *tapu*. They were the *Maori* national Gods, for they were their common ancestors. But at the same time

* Hecuba, l. 533–9.

every *Maori* tribe and family invoked independently each its own tribal and family ancestors, just as was the practice of the Greeks and Latins.

CHAPTER II.

MAORI COSMOGONY AND MYTHOLOGY.

An quoquam genitos nisi Cœlo credere fas est
Esse homines.—*Manilius.*

THE *Maori* had no tradition of the Creation. The
great mysterious Cause of all things existing in the
Cosmos was, as he conceived it, the generative Power.
Commencing with a primitive state of Darkness, he
conceived Po (=Night) as a person capable of beget-
ting a race of beings resembling itself. After a
succession of several generations of the race of Po,
Te Ata (=Morn) was given birth to. Then followed
certain beings existing when Cosmos was without
form, and void. Afterwards came Rangi (=Heaven),
Papa (=Earth), the Winds, and other Sky powers,
as are recorded in the genealogical traditions preserved to the present time.

We have reason to consider the mythological traditions of the *Maori* as dating from a very antient
period. They are held to be very sacred, and not
to be repeated except in places set apart as sacred.

The Genealogies recorded hereafter are divisible into
three distinct epochs :—

1. That comprising the personified Powers of Nature
preceding the existence of man, which Powers are
regarded by the *Maori* as their own primitive ancestors,
and are invoked in their *karakia* by all the *Maori* race ;

for we find the names of Rangi, Rongo, Tangaroa, &c.,
mentioned as *Atua* or Gods of the *Maori* of the Sandwich Islands and other Islands of the Pacific inhabited
by the same race. The common worship of these
primitive *Atua* constituted the National religion of the
Maori.

2. In addition to this the *Maori* had a religious
worship peculiar to each tribe and to each family, in
forms of *karakia* or invocation addressed to the spirits
of dead ancestors of their own proper line of descent.

Ancestral spirits who had lived in the flesh before the
migration to New Zealand would be invoked by all the
tribes in New Zealand, so far as their names had been
preserved, in their traditional records as mighty spirits.

3. From the time of the migration to New Zealand
each tribe and each family would in addition address
their invocations to their own proper line of ancestors,—
thus giving rise to a family religious worship in addition
to the national religion.

The cause of the preservation of their Genealogies
becomes intelligible when we consider that they often
formed the ground-work of their religious formulas,
and that to make an error or even hesitation in repeating
a *karakia* was deemed fatal to its efficacy.

In the forms of *karakia* addressed to the spirits of
ancestors, the concluding words are generally a petition
to the *Atua* invoked to give force or effect to the *karakia*
as being derived through the *Tipua*, the *Pukenga*, and
the *Whananga*, and so descending to the living *Tauira*.

MAORI COSMOGONY.

Powers of Night and Darkness.	Te Po (=The Night). Te Po-teki (=hanging Night). Te Po-terea (=drifting Night). Te Po-whawha (=moaning Night). Hine-ruakimoe Te Po.
Powers of Light.	Te Ata (=The Morn). Te Ao-tu-roa (=The abiding Day). Te Ao-marama (=bright Day). Whaitua (=space).
Powers of Cosmos without form and void.	Te Kore (=The Void). Te Kore-tuatahi. Te Kore-tuarua. Kore-nui. Kore-roa. Kore-para. Kore-whiwhia. Kore-rawea. Kore-te-tamaua (=Void fast bound). Te Mangu (=the black) sc. Erebus.

From the union of Te Mangu with Mahorahora-nui-a-Rangi (=The great expanse of Rangi) came four children :—

1. Toko-mua (=elder prop).
2. Toko-roto (=middle prop).
3. Toko-pa (=last prop).
4. Rangi-potiki (=child Rangi).

GENEALOGICAL DESCENT FROM TOKO-MUA.

Powers of The Air, Winds.	Tu-awhio-nuku (=Tu of the whirl-wind).
	Tu-awhio-rangi.
	Paroro-tea (=white skud).
	Hau-tuia (=piercing wind).
	Hau-ngangana (blustering wind).
	Ngana.
	Ngana-nui.
	Ngana-roa.
	Ngana-ruru.
	Ngana-mawaki.
	Tapa-huru-kiwi.
	Tapa-huru-manu.
	* Tiki.
Human beings begin to exist.	Tiki-te-pou-mua (The 1st Man).
	Tiki-te-pou-roto.
	Tiki-haohao.
	Tiki-ahu-papa.
	Te Papa-tutira.
	Ngai.
	Ngai-nui.
	Ngai-roa.
	Ngai-peha.
	Te Atitutu.
	Te Ati-hapai.
	† Toi-te-huatahi.
	Rauru.
	Rutana.

* Whose wife was Hine-titamauri de quâ infra.
† Whose wife was Puhaorangi de quâ infra.

Whatonga.
Apa-apa.
Taha-titi.
Ruatapu.
Rakeora.
Tama-ki-te-ra.
Rongo-maru-a-whatu.
Rere.
Tăta=

Wakaotirangi.	Rongokako.
Hotumatapu.	Tamatea.
Motai.	*Kahu-hunu.
Ue.	
Raka.	
Kakati.	
Tawhao.	
Turongo.	
Raukawa.	
Wakatere.	
Taki-hiku.	
Tama-te-hura.	
Tui-tao.	
Hae.	
Nga-tokowaru.	

* Tamatea was settled at Muriwhenua, and his son Kahuhunu was
born there. The latter went on a journey to Nukutauraua
near the Mahia, and there married Rongomai-wahine, having
got rid of her husband Tamatakutai by craft. Tamatea went
to bring him home, but on their return their canoe was upset
in a rapid, near where the river Waikato flows out of the lake
Taupo, and Tamatea was drowned.

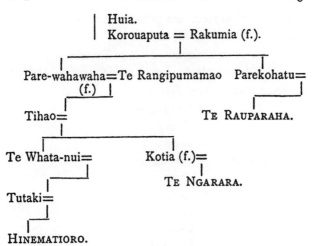

GENEALOGICAL DESCENT FROM TOKO-ROTO.

	Rangi-nui.
	Rangi-roa.
	Rangi-pouri.
	Rangi-potango.
Powers	Rangi-whetu-ma.
of the	Rangi-whekere.
Heavens.	Ao-nui.
	Ao-roa.
	Ao-tara.
	Urupa.
	Hoehoe.
	Puhaorangi (f.).

After the birth of Rauru, the son of Toi-te-huatahi and Kuraemonoa, while Toi was absent from home fishing, Puhaorangi came down from Heaven, and

carried off Kuraemonoa to be his own wife. She bore
four children from this union :—

    1. Ohomairangi.   *2.* Tawhirioho.
    3. Ohotaretare.   *4.* Oho-mata-kamokamo.

From Ohomairangi descended :—

	Muturangi.
	Taunga.
	Tuamatua.
Time of	Houmaitahiti.
Migration	Tama-te-kapua.
from	Kahu.
Hawaiki.	Tawaki.
	Uenuku.
	Rangitihi.
	Ratorua.
	Wakairikawa.
	Waitapu.
	Hine-rehua.
	Te Kahu-reremoa.
	Waitapu.
	Parekawa.
	Te Kohera.
	Pakaki =

Te Rangi-pumamao=   Parewahaika=Te Whata

Tihao.	Tokoahu.	Tuiri.
Kotia.	Hihitaua.	Waho (f.).
TE NGARARA.	Te Tumuhuia	TE HIRA.
	or	
	TARAIA.	

GENEALOGICAL DESCENT FROM TOKO-PA.

Kohu (=Mist) was the child of Tokopa.

Kohu married Te Ika-roa (=The Milky-way), and gave birth to Nga Whetu (=The Stars).

GENEALOGICAL DESCENT FROM RANGI-POTIKI.

Rangi-potiki had three wives, the first of which was Hine-ahu-papa; from her descended :—

Sky Powers.	Tu-nuku.
	Tu-rangi.
	Tama-i-koropao.
	Haronga.

Haronga took to wife Tongo-tongo. Their children were a son and daughter, Te Ra (=The Sun) and Marama (=The Moon). Haronga perceiving that there was no light for his daughter Marama, gave Te Kohu in marriage to Te Ikaroa, and the Stars were born to give light for the sister of Te Ra, for the child of Tongo-tongo. "*Nga tokorua a Tongo-tongo*" (= the two children of Tongotongo) is a proverbial term for the Sun and Moon at the present day.

Rangi-potiki's second wife was Papatuanuku. She gave birth to the following children :—

Rehua (a star).
Rongo.
Tangaroa.
Tahu.
Punga and Here, twins.
Hua and Ari,   do.

C

Nukumera　　　　⎫
　　　　　　　　⎬ twins.
Rango-maraeroa　⎭

Marere-o-tonga　⎫
　　　　　　　　⎬ do.
Takataka-putea　⎭

Tu-matauenga　　⎫
　　　　　　　　⎬ do.
Tu-potiki　　　　⎭

RONGO was *atua* of the *kumara*.

TANGAROA was ancestor of Fish and the *Pounamu*, which is classed with fish by the *Maori*. Tangaroa took to wife Te Anu-matao (=the chilly cold): from which union descended.

All of the Fish Class.	Te Whata-uira-a-tangaroa. Te Whatukura. Poutini. Te Pounamu.

TAHU was *atua* presiding over peace and feasts.

PUNGA was ancestor of the lizard, shark, and ill-favoured creatures: hence the proverb *"aitanga-a-Punga"* (=child of Punga) to denote an ugly fellow.

TU-MATAUENGA was the *Maori* war God.

Rangi-potiki's third wife was Papa (=Earth). Tangaroa was accused of having committed adultery with Papa, and Rangipotiki, armed with his spear, went to obtain satisfaction. He found Tangaroa seated by the door of his house, who, when he saw Rangi thus coming towards him, began the following *karakia*, at the same time striking his right shoulder with his left hand:—

Tangaroa, Tangaroa,
Tangaroa, unravel;
Unravel the tangle,
Unravel, untwist.

> Though Rangi is distant,
> He is to be reached.
> Some darkness for above,
> Some light for below
> Freely give
> For bright Day[1]

This invocation of Tangaroa was scarce ended when Rangi made a thrust at him. Tangaroa warded it off, and it missed him. Then Tangaroa made a thrust at Rangi, and pierced him quite through the thigh, and he fell.

While Rangi lay wounded he begat his child Kueo (=Moist). The cause of this name was Rangi's wetting his couch while he lay ill of his wound. After Kueo, he begat Mimi-ahi, so-called from his making water by the fireside. Next he begat Tane-tuturi (=straight-leg-Tane), so-called because Rangi could now stretch his legs. Afterwards he begat Tane-pepeki (=bent-leg-Tane), so-called because Rangi could sit with his knees bent. The next child was Tane-ua-tika (=straight-neck Tane), for Rangi's neck was now straight, and he could hold up his head. The next child born was called Tane-ua-ha[2] (=strong-neck-Tane), for Rangi's neck was strong. Then was born Tane-te-waiora (=lively Tane), so called because Rangi was quite recovered. Then was born Tane-nui-a-Rangi (=Tane great son of Rangi). And last of all was born Paea, a daughter. She was the last

---

[1] This *karakia* is the most antient example of the kind. It is now applied as suggestive of a peaceable settlement of a quarrel.

[2] Ha=kaha.

of Rangi's children. With Paea they came to an end, so she was named Paea, which signifies ' closed.'

Some time after the birth of these children the thought came to Tane-nui-a-Rangi to separate their father from them. Tane had seen the light of the Sun shining under the armpit of Rangi; so he consulted with his elder brothers what they should do. They all said, "Let us kill our father, because he has shut us up in darkness, and let us leave our mother for our parent." But Tane advised, "Do not let us kill our father, but rather let us raise him up above, so that there may be light." To this they consented; so they prepared ropes, and when Rangi was sound asleep they rolled him over on the ropes, and Paea took him on her back. Two props were also placed under Rangi. The names of the props were Tokohurunuku, and Tokohururangi. Then lifting him with the aid of these two props, they shoved him upwards. Then Papa thus uttered her farewell to Rangi.

"*Haera ra, e Rangi, ē! ko te wehenga taua i a Rangi.*"
"Go, O Rangi, alas! for my separation from Rangi."
And Rangi answered from above:
"*Heikona ra, e Papa, ē! ko te wehenga taua i a Papa.*"
"Remain there, O Papa. Alas! for my separation from Papa."

So Rangi dwelt above, and Tane and his brothers dwelt below with their mother, Papa.

Some time after this Tane desired to have his mother Papa for his wife. But Papa said, "Do not turn your inclination towards me, for evil will come to you. Go to your ancestor Mumuhango." So Tane took

Mumuhango to wife, who brought forth the *totara*
tree. Tane returned to his mother dissatisfied, and
his mother said, "Go to your ancestor Hine-tu-a-
maunga (=the mountain maid)." So Tane took
Hine-tu-a-maunga to wife, who conceived, but did not
bring forth a child. Her offspring was the rusty water
of mountains, and the monster reptiles common to
mountains. Tane was displeased, and returned to his
mother. Papa said to him "Go to your ancestor
Rangahore." So Tane went, and took that female for a
wife, who brought forth stone. This greatly displeased
Tane, who again went back to Papa. Then Papa said
"Go to your ancestor Ngaore (=the tender one). Tane
took Ngaore to wife. And Ngaore gave birth to the *toetoe*
(a species of rush-like grass). Tane returned to his
mother in displeasure. She next advised him, "Go to
your ancestor Pakoti." Tane did as he was bid, but Pakoti
only brought forth *harekeke* (=phormium tenax). Tane
had a great many other wives at his mother's bidding,
but none of them pleased him, and his heart was greatly
troubled, because no child was born to give birth to
Man; so he thus addressed his mother—"Old lady,
there will never be any progeny for me." Thereupon
Papa said, "Go to your ancestor, Ocean, who is
grumbling there in the distance. When you reach
the beach at Kura-waka, gather up the earth in the form
of man." So Tane went and scraped up the earth at
Kura-waka. He gathered up the earth, the body was
formed, and then the head, and the arms; then he joined
on the legs, and patted down the surface of the
belly, so as to give the form of man ; and when he had
done this, he returned to his mother and said, "The

whole body of the man is finished." Thereupon his
mother said, " Go to your ancestor Mauhi, she will
give the *raho*.[1]   Go to your ancestor Whete, she will give
the *timutimu*.[2] Go to your ancestor Taua-ki-te-marangai,
she will give the *paraheka*.[3] Go to your ancestor Pungaheko, she has the *huruhuru*." So Tane went to these
female ancestors, who gave him the things asked for.
He then went to Kura-waka. Katahi ka whakanoho ia i
nga raho ki roto i nga kuwha o te wahine i hanga ki
te one: Ka mau era. Muri atu ka whakanoho ia ko
te timutimu na Whete i homai ki waenga i nga raho;
muri atu ko te paraheka na Taua-ki-te-marangai i
homai ka whakanoho ki te take o te timutimu : muri
iho ko te huruhuru na Pungaheko i homai ka whakanoho ki runga i te puke. Ka oti, katahi ka tapa ko
Hineahuone. Then he named this female form Hine-
ahu-one (=The earth formed maid).

Tane took Hine-ahu-one to wife. She first gave birth
to Tiki-tohua—the egg of a bird from which have
sprung all the birds of the air. After that, Tiki-
kapakapa was born—a female. Then first was born for
Tane a human child. Tane took great care of Tiki-
kapakapa, and when she grew up he gave her a new
name, Hine-a-tauira (=the pattern maid). Then he
took her to wife, and she bore a female child who was
named Hine-titamauri.

One day Hine-a-tauira said to Tane, " Who is my
father?" Tane laughed. A second time Hine-a-tauira
asked the same question. Then Tane made a sign:[4]

---

[1] [2] [3] Quaedam partes corporis genitales.

[4] *Katahi ka tohungia e Tane ki tona ure.*

and the woman understood, and her heart was dark, and she gave herself up to mourning, and fled away to Rikiriki, and to Naonao, to Rekoreko, to Waewae-te-Po, and to Po.[1] The woman fled away, hanging down her head. [2] Then she took the name of Hine-nui-te-Po (=great woman of Night). Her farewell words to Tane were—"Remain, O Tane, to pull up our offspring to Day; while I go below to drag down our offspring to Night."[3]

Tane sorrowed for his daughter-wife, and cherished his daughter Hinetitamauri; and when she grew up he gave her to Tiki to be his wife, and their first-born child was Tiki-te-pou-mua.[4]

The following narrative is a continuation of the history of Hinenuitepo from another source:—

After Hinenuitepo fled away to her ancestors in the realms of Night, she gave birth to Te Po-uriuri (=The Dark one), and to Te Po-tangotango (=The very dark), and afterwards to Pare-koritawa, who married Tawaki, one of the race of Rangi. Hence the proverb when the sky is seen covered with small clouds " *Parekoritawa is tilling her garden.*" When Tawaki climbed to Heaven with Parekoritawa, he repeated this *karakia* :—

> Ascend, O Tawaki, by the narrow path,
> By which the path of Rangi was followed ;
> The path of Tu-kai-te-uru.

---

[1] These were all ancestors of the race of Powers of Night.

[2] *He oti, ka rere te wahine : ka anga ko te pane ki raro, tuwhera tonu nga kuwha, hamama tonu te puapua.*

[3] "*Heikona, e Tane, hei kukume ake ı a taua hua ki te Ao ; kia haere au ki raro hei kukume iho i a taua hua ki te Po.*"

[4] Vid. Genealogical Table.

The narrow path is climbed,
The broad path is climbed,
The path by which was followed
Your ancestors, Te Aonui,
Te Ao-roa,
Te Ao-whititera.
Now you mount up
To your *Ihi*,
To your *Mana*,
To the Thousands above,
To your *Ariki*,
To your *Tapairu*,
To your *Pukenga*,
To your *Whananga*,
To your *Tauira*.

When Tawaki and Parekoritawa mounted to the Sky, they left behind them a token—a black moth—a token of the mortal body.

Pare gave birth to Uenuku (=Rainbow). Afterwards she brought forth Whatitiri (=Thunder). Hence the rainbow in the sky, and the thunder-clap.

CHAPTER III.

RELIGIOUS RITES OF THE MAORI.

Ἀλλ' ἄγε δὴ τινα μάντιν ἐρείομεν.—Hom. Il. 1-62.

THE religious rites and ceremonies of the *Maori* were strange and complex, and must have been a severe burden, as will be understood from the translations of *Maori* narratives relating to such matters contained in these pages. To make these translations more intelligible to the reader, a brief review of the subject is now given in explanation.

The religious rites under consideration are immediately connected with certain laws relating to things *tapu*, or things sacred and prohibited, the breach of which laws by anyone is a crime displeasing to the *Atua* of his family. Anything *tapu* must not be allowed to come in contact with any vessel or place where food is kept. This law is absolute. Should such contact take place, the food, the vessel, or place, become *tapu*, and only a few very sacred persons, themselves *tapu*, dare to touch these things.

The idea in which this law originated appears to have been that a portion of the sacred essence of an *Atua*, or of a sacred person, was directly communicable to objects which they touched, and also that the sacredness so communicated to any object could afterwards be more or less retransmitted to anything else brought into contact with it. It was therefore necessary that anything containing the sacred essence of an *Atua* should be made *tapu* to protect it from being polluted by the

contact of food designed to be eat; for the act of
eating food which had touched anything *tapu*, involved
the necessity of eating the sacredness of the *Atua*, from
whom it derived its sacredness.

It seems that the practice of cannibalism must have
had a close connexion with such a system of belief.
To eat an enemy was the greatest degradation to
which he could be subjected, and so it must have been
regarded as akin to blasphemy to eat anything containing a particle of divine essence.

Everything not included under the class *tapu* was
called *noa*, meaning free or common.   Things and
persons *tapu* could, however, be made *noa* by means of
certain ceremonies, the object of which was to extract
the *tapu* essence, and restore it to the source whence it
originally came.   It has been already stated that every
tribe and every family has its own especial *Atua*.   The
Ariki, or head of a family, in both male and female
lines, are regarded by their own family with a veneration almost equal to that of their *Atua*.[1]   They form, as

---

[1] It is observable that Homer attributes special honor to a few of
his heroes, who appear to have been the male representatives of
their race,—as to Agamemnon of the race of Pelops, and to
Aeneas of the race of Assaracus.   With respect to each of
them, it is mentioned that he was honored as a God by his
people.   " Θεὸς δ' ὣς τίετο δήμῳ."   Among the Maori these
chiefs would have been distinguished by the title of *Ariki*.
Homer gives them the title "ἄναξ ἀνδρῶν," the old meaning of
which words has been a matter of much inquiry.   Mr Gladstone
(Homer and Homeric Age, vol. I. p. 456) says, "It seems to
me that this restraint in the use of the name 'ἄναξ ἀνδρῶν' was
not unconnected with a sense of reverence towards it;" and he
suggests the word chieftain as its fit representative.   Might not
its original meaning have been similar to that of *Ariki?*

it were, the connecting links between the living and the spirits of the dead; and the ceremonies required for releasing anything from the *tapu* state cannot be perfected without their intervention.

On arriving one evening at a *Maori* settlement, I found that a ceremony, in which everyone appeared to take deep interest, was to take place in the morning. The inhabitants were mostly professing Christians, and the old sacred place of the settlement was, from the increase of their numbers, inconveniently near their houses; a part of it was, therefore, required to be added to the *Pa*. I was curious to see in what way the land required would be made *noa*. In the morning when I went to the place I found a numerous assembly, while in the centre of the space was a large native oven, from which women were removing the earth and mat-coverings. When opened it was seen to contain only *kumara*, or sweet potato. One of these was offered to each person present, which was held in the hand while the usual morning service was read, concluding with a short prayer that God's blessing might rest on the place. After this each person ate his *kumara*, and the place was declared to be *noa*. I could not but think that the native teacher had done wisely in thus adopting so much of old ceremonial as to satisfy the scruples of those of little faith. In this case, every one present, by eating food cooked on the *tapu* ground, equally incurred the risk of offending the *Atua* of the family, which risk was believed to be removed by the Christian *karakia*.

By neglecting the laws of *tapu*, *Ariki*, chiefs, and

other sacred persons are especially liable to the displeasure of their *Atua*, and are therefore afraid to do a
great many ordinary acts necessary in private life. For
this reason a person of the sacred class was obliged to
eat his meals in the open air, at a little distance from
his sacred dwelling, and from the place which he and
his friends usually occupied; and if he could not eat
all that had been placed before him he kept the
remainder for his own sole use, in a sacred place
appropriated for that purpose: for no one dared to
eat what so sacred a person had touched.

The term *karakia* is applicable to all forms of prayer
to the *Atua*: but there are a variety of names or titles
to denote *karakia* having special objects. The translations of those now presented to the reader will, it is
believed, speak for themselves as to the nature of *Maori*
worship, and carry with them a more clear and full con-
viction as to what it really was than any mere statements
however faithful. It will be seen that a *karakia* is in
some cases very like a prayer,—in other cases for the
most part an invocation of spirits of ancestors in genealogical order,—in other cases a combination of prayer
and invocation.

THE KARAKIA OF HINETEIWAIWA.

Said to have been used at the birth of her son Tuhuruhuru. It is of great antiquity, dating from a time
long anterior to the migration to New Zealand.

Weave, weave the mat,
Couch for my unborn child,
Qui lectus aquâ inundabitur:
Rupe, et manumea inundabuntur:
Lectus meus, et mei fetûs inundabitur:

Inundabor aquâ, inundabor;
Maritus meus inundabitur.[1]
Now I step upon (the mat).
The *Matitikura*[2] to Rupe above,
    *   *   *   Toroa   *
    *   *   *   Takapu   *
    *   *   *   to cause to be born,
My child now one with myself.
Stand firm *turuturu*[3] of Hine-rauwharangi,
    *   *   *   *   Hine-teiwaiwa,
Stand by your *tia*,[4] Ihuwareware,
Stand by your *kona*,[5] Ihuatamai,
Chide me not in my trouble,
Me Hine-teiwaiwa, O Rupe.[6]
Release from above your hair,[7]
Your head, your shoulders,
Your breast, your liver,
Your knees, your feet,
Let them come forth.
The old lady[8] with night-dark visage,
She will make you stretch,
She will make you rise up.
Let go *ewe*,[9] let go *take*,[10]
Let go *parapara*.[11] Come forth.

---

[1] Hæc ad effusionem aquarum sub tempus partûs spectant.

[2] The name of a powerful *karakia*.

[3] *Turuturu*, a sharp pointed prop, two of which are fixed in the floor to serve as a frame for weaving mats—also used by women in child-birth to hold by.

[4] [5] Names of lower parts of abdomen.

[6] Rupe or Maui-mua, brother-in-law of Hine-teiwaiwa.

[7] Addressed to the unborn child.

[8] The old lady referred to was Hine-nui-te-po, the mother of the female ancestress of mankind.

[9] [10] [11] Names of different parts of the decidua.

For tradition as to Tuhuruhuru and other names here mentioned vid. Sir Geo. Grey's "Mythology and Traditions of New Zealand," p. 39 et seq.

This *karakia* is still in use with the Arawa tribe in cases of difficult parturition. When such cases occur, it is concluded that the woman has committed some fault—some breach of the *tapu*, which is to be discovered by the *matakite* (=seer). The father of the child then plunges in the river, while the *karakia* is being repeated, and the child will generally be born ere ever he returns.

The following form of *karakia* is also used by members of the same tribe in similar cases:—

> O! Hine-teiwaiwa, release Tuhuruhuru,
> O! Rupe, release your nephew.

The ancestors of the father of the child are then invoked by name. First the elder male line of ancestors, commencing with an ancestor who lived in Hawaiki and terminating with the living representative of that line. Then follows a repetition of the ancestral line next in succession, and the third in succession, if the child be not born.[1] After which the *tohunga* addressing the unborn child says, "Come forth. The fault rests with me. Come forth." The *tohunga* continues thus—

> Unravel the tangle, unravel the crime,
> Untie *manuka*, let it be loosed.
> Distant though Rangi,
> He is reached.

If the child be not now born, Tiki is invoked thus—

> Tiki of the heap of earth,
> Tiki scraped together,
> When hands and feet were formed,
> First produced at Hawaiki.

---

[1] In the *Maori* MS., of which the above is a translation, the names of the ancestors of the chief of the tribe referred to are given in genealogical order, but are omitted here.

If the child be a male, it will be born—if a female, the mother's line of ancestors must be invoked.

Intimately connected with the superstition respecting things *tapu* is the belief as to the cause of disease, namely, that a spirit has taken possession of the body of the sufferer. The belief is that any neglect of the law of *tapu*, either wilful, or accidental, or even brought about by the act of another person, causes the anger of the *Atua* of the family who punishes the offender by sending some infant spirit to feed on a part of his body — infant spirits being generally selected for this office on account of their love of mischief, and because not having lived long enough on earth to form attachments to their living relatives, they are less likely to show them mercy. When, therefore, a person falls sick, and cannot remember that he has himself broken any law of the *tapu*, he has to consult a *matakite* (seer) and a *tohunga* to discover the crime, and use the proper ceremonies to appease the *Atua;* for there is in practice a method of making a person offend against the laws of *tapu* without his being aware of it. This method is a secret one called *makutu*. It is sufficient for a person who knows this art, if he can obtain a portion of the spittle of his enemy, or some leavings from his food, in order that he may treat it in a manner sure to bring down the resentment of his family *Atua*. For this reason a person would not dare to spit when in the presence of anyone he feared might be disposed to injure him, if he had a reputation for skill in this evil art.

With such a belief as to the cause of all disease it will not be wondered at that the treatment of it was

confined to the *karakia* of a *tohunga* or wise man.
One or two examples of such cases will be sufficient
to explain this as well as to show the in-rooted superstition of the *Maori*.

When anyone becomes *porangi* or insane, as not
unfrequently happens, he is taken to a *tohunga*, who
first makes an examination as to the cause of the
disease. He and the sick man then go to the water-
side, and the *tohunga*, stripping off his own clothes,
takes in his hand an obsidian flint. First he cuts a
lock of hair from the left side of the sick man's head, and
afterwards a lock of hair from the top of his head. The
obsidian flint is then placed on the ground, and upon it
the lock of hair which had been cut from the left side
of the head. The lock of hair cut from the top of
the head is held aloft in the left hand of the *tohunga*,
while in his right hand he holds a common stone,
which is also raised aloft, while the following *karakia*
is being repeated by him.

> Tu, divide, Tu, split,
> This is the *waiapu* flint,
> Now about to cry aloud
> To the Moon of ill-omen.

Then the *tohunga* breathes on the flint, and smashes
it with the stone held in his right hand. After this he
selects a shoot of the plant *toetoe*, and pulls it up, and
then fastens to it both the locks of hair. Then diving
in the river, he lets go the *toetoe* and locks of hair, and
when they float on the surface of the water, he commences his great *karakia* thus—

> This is the *Tiri* of Tu-i-rawea,
> This is the *Tiri* of Uenuku.

Where lies your fault ?
Was eating a *kutu* your fault ?
Was sitting on *tapu* ground your fault ?
Unravel the tangle,
Unravel, untie.
Take away the fault from the head
Of the *Atua* who afflicts this man.
Take away the disease,
And the *mana* of the curser.
Turn your *mana* against your *tohunga*,
And your *whaiwhaia*.[1]
Give me the curse
To make as cooked food.
Your *Atua* desecrated,
Your *tapu*, your curse,
Your sacred-place-dwelling *Atua*,
Your house-dwelling *Atua*,
Give me to cook for food.
Your *tapu* is desecrated by me.
The rays of the sun,
The brave of the world,
The *mana*, give me.
Let your *Atua*, and your *tapu*
Be food for me to eat.
Let the head of the curser
Be baked in the oven,
Served up for food for me
Dead, and gone to Night.

The latter part of this *karakia* is a curse directed against some *tohunga* supposed to have caused the disease by his art of *makutu*.

Makutu was the weapon of the weak, who had no other mode of obtaining redress. There is no doubt but that it exercised a restraining influence, in a

---

[1] A *karakia* so called.

D

society where no law but that of force generally
prevailed, as a check to theft and unjust dealing
generally ; for there is among the *Maori* a firm
belief in and dread of its power. This is very
evident from the following account given by one of
themselves of the mode employed to detect and
punish a petty theft.

A woman is much vexed when any of the flax
scraped by her is stolen, and she consults a *tohunga*,
in order to discover the thief. Whether the flax has
been stolen from her house or from the water, the
woman's house must be *tapu*. No one must be
allowed to enter it. This is necessary, that the
makutu may take effect, and the person who stole
the flax be discovered. So when the woman comes
to the *tohunga* he first asks her " Has any one entered
your house?" She replies " No." Then the *tohunga*
bids her return home, saying "I will come to you at
night." The woman returns home, and at night the
tohunga comes to her. He bids her point out her
house, and then goes with her to the water side.
Having taken off his clothes, he strikes the water
with a stick or wand, brought with him for that purpose, and immediately the form of the thief stands
before them. The *tohunga* thus curses it—

> May your eyes look at the moon—
> Eyes of flax be yours,
> Hands of flax be yours,
> Feet of flax be yours.
> Let your hands snatch
> At the rays of the Sun.
> Let your hands snatch at Whiro,
> Whiro in vast heaven,

Whiro born of Papa.
Snatch, snatch at your own head,
Perishing in the Night of Darkness,
In the Night of Death—Death.

WHAKAHOKITU

Is the name given to forms of *makutu* employed to counteract the curse of some other *tohunga*, or wise-man; for whoever practises *makutu*, even though he be skilled in the art, may have to yield to the *mana* of some other wise-man who can command the assistance of a more powerful *Atua*. The following is a specimen of this kind of *makutu*—

Great curse, long curse,
Great curse, binding curse,
Binding your sacredness
To the tide of destruction.
Come hither, sacred spell,
To be looked on by me.
Cause the curser to lie low
In gloomy Night, in dark Night,
In the Night of ill-omen.
Great wind, lasting wind,
Changing wind of *Rangi* above.
He falls. He perishes.
Cause to waste away the curser *tohunga*.
Let him bite the oven-stones.
Be food for me,
The *tapu* and the *mana*,
Of your *Atua*,
Of your *karakia*,
Of your *tohunga*.

Among the *Atua* much held in awe by the *Maori* were the *Atua noho-whare*, or house-dwelling gods—spirits of the germs of unborn infants. They are also known by the name *kahukahu*, the meaning of which word was explained in a former publication.

The *Maori* has also a firm belief in omens derived from dreams, and from any sudden movements of the body or limbs during sleep, all which signs are believed to be warnings from the *Atua*.

There is a class of dreams called *moe-papa*, which are very unlucky: and if any one has one of these dreams, he will avoid going on a projected journey; for it is firmly believed that should he persist in going he will fall into an enemy's ambush, or meet with some other misfortune. Hence the proverbial remark, if a person has neglected such a warning, and has fallen in with a war-party, " He was warned by a *moe-papa*, and yet went." The kind of sleep denoted by this word is described to be the climbing a precipice, the wandering astray in a forest, entering a house, climbing a tree. Such dreams are death warnings. They appear to be such as we term night-mare.

The startings of the limbs or body during sleep are called *takiri*, some of which are lucky, and some unlucky, each kind being distinguished by a special name.

The lucky *takiri* are—

The *hokai*, or starting of the leg or foot in a forward direction. It denotes the repulse of the enemy.

The *tauaro*, or starting of the arm towards the body.

The *whakaara*, when in sleep the head starts upwards. It signifies that ere long the *Ariki* or his father will arrive.

The *kapo*, a very lucky sign. While a man sleeps with

his right arm for a pillow, if the arm starts so as to strike his head, on awaking he will not mention it to his companions; for he knows by this omen that in the next battle which takes place it will be his good fortune to kill the first man of the enemy.

The unlucky *takiri* are—

The *kohera*, a starting of the arm and leg of one side of the body in an outward direction.

The *peke*, a starting of the arm outwards from the body.

The *whawhati*, a sleep in which the legs, the neck, and the head are bent doubled up towards the belly. This is very unlucky. The evil will not come to another person, but attends the man himself.

The former *takiri* do not necessarily denote evil to the individual sleeper, but to any of his companions.

CHAPTER IV.

RELIGIOUS RITES OF THE MAORI.

Tantum Relligio potuit suadere.—Lucretius.

YOU ask me about the customs of *Maori* men, and their origin, how men came to learn them. This is the source whence men learnt them. Their knowledge is not from modern times. Papa, Rangi, Tiki were the first to give rules to men for work of all kinds, for killing, for man-eating, for *karakia*. In former days the knowledge of the *Maori* was great, in all matters, from this teaching, and so men learnt how to set rules for this thing and for that thing. Hence came the ceremony of *Pure* for the dead, the *karakia* for the new-born infant, for grown men, for battle, for storming a *Pa*, for eels, for birds, for *makutu*, and a multitude of other *karakia*. Tiki was the source from which they came down to the *tupua*, the *pukenga*, the *wananga*, and the *tauira*. The men of antient days are a source of invocation for the *tauira*. Hence the *karakia* had its power, and came down from one generation to another ever having power. Formerly their *karakia* gave men power. From the time when the *Rongo-pai* (=Gospel) arrived here, and men were no longer *tapu*, disease commenced. The man of former days was not afflicted by disease. He died only when bent by age. He died when he came to the natural end of life.

My writing to you begins with the *karakia* for a mother when her breasts give no milk. After a child is born, if the mother's breasts have no milk, her husband goes for the *tohunga*. When the *tohunga* arrives the mother and child are carried to the water-side, and the *tohunga* dipping a handful of weed in the water, sprinkles it on the mother. The child is taken away from the mother by the *tohunga*, who then repeats this *karakia*:—

Water-springs from above give me,
To pour on the breast of this woman.
Dew of Heaven give me,
To cause to trickle the breast of this woman;
At the points of the breast of this woman;
Breasts flowing with milk,
Flowing to the points of the breast of this woman,
Milk in plenty yielding.
For now the infant cries and moans,
In the great night, in the long night.
Tu the benefactor,
Tu the giver,
Tu the bountiful,
Come to me, to this *tauira*.

After this the child is dipped in the water, and the mother and child are kept apart. One whole night they are kept apart, in order that the *karakia* may take effect. The mother remains alone in her house, while the *tohunga* seated outside it repeats his *karakia*. The *tohunga* also instructs the woman thus—"If the points of your breasts begin to itch, lay open your clothes, and lie naked." Some time after her breasts begin to itch, and the woman knows that the *karakia* is taking effect. Afterwards her breasts become painful, and she calls out to the *tohunga* "my breasts itch and are painful, they are full of milk." Then the child is brought to the mother. See what power the *karakia* of the *Maori* possessed.

This is a word, a thought of mine. There has not

been any remarkable sign of late years, from the time
of the arrival of the Rongo-pai (=Gospel), like the
signs seen in this island when men were *tapu*, when
karakia had power. One sign seen in this island was
the Ra-kutia (=the closed sun). At mid-day there was
darkness, and the stars were seen. After two hours
perhaps of darkness, daylight returned. Our fathers
saw this sign : but there are now no signs like those of
former days.

CEREMONY OF TUA.

When a male child is born to a Chief, all his tribe
rejoice. The mother is separated from the inhabitants
of the settlement, to prevent her coming in contact
with persons engaged in cultivating the *kumara*, lest
anything belonging to the mother should be accidentally
touched by them, lest the *kumara* should be affected by
her state of *tapu* ; for the sacredness of any *rehu-wahine*
is greatly feared.

When the child is about a month old, and strives with
its hands to reach its mother's breast, the ceremony of
Tūa takes place. Two fires are kindled ; one fire for the
Ariki, one fire for the *Atua*. The food to be cooked on
the fire is fern-root. Then the *tohunga* takes the child
in his arms, and repeats this *karakia* :—

> Breathe quick thy lung,
> A healthy lung.
> Breathe strong thy long,
> A firm lung,
> A brave lung.
> Severing[1] for your bravery,
>   *   * tilling food,

---

[1] The severing of umbilical cord is here referred to.

Severing for wielding the weapon,
    *   * warding off,
    *   * seizing the first man,
    *   * storming the *Pa*.
  &c.   &c.
  &c.   &c.
The boy infant is stept[1] over,
    * * * * climbed[1] over,
    * * * * lifted in the arms,
The boy infant is free from *tapu*,
He runs freely where food is cooked.
Cause this *karakia* to flow gently,
To the *Pukenga*,
To the *Wananga*,
To the *Tauira*.

When this *karakia* ends the ceremony of *Poipoi*
(=waving) follows. The *tohunga* takes up the fern-root
cooked for the *Atua*, and waving it over the child
repeats these words:—"This is for the *Tipua*, for the
Pukenga, for the *Wananga*. Eat it. It is the food
cooked for you to eat." The cooked fern-root is
then deposited on the sacred place. Afterwards
the child is taken in the arms of the female *Ariki*, who
waves over it the fern-root cooked on her fire, and
touches with it different parts of the child's body. The
Ariki is said then to eat this fern-root, but does not
do so in fact. She only spits on it, and throws it on
the sacred place.

If there are several female *Ariki* of the same family
of whom one is absent, a figure is made with weeds to
represent her. Then part of the fern-root is offered to

---

[1] The female *Ariki* at these words steps over the child, and then
takes it in her arms.

the figure and is stuck in it. All these ceremonies take place on sacred ground. The part of the ceremony—that of touching the body of the child with the food to be eat by the *Ariki*—is named *kai-katoa*. After this the child is free from *tapu*, so that persons of the family may take it in their arms.

No further ceremony takes place till the child arrives at youth, when his hair is cut, and the young person is released from *tapu*. The hair must be cut in the morning in order to insure a strict observance of *tapu*; for it is not only the *tohunga* who must be *tapu* on this occasion, but also the whole tribe. This *tapu* commences in the morning, and no one must eat food while it lasts. Should any one eat during that time it will be discovered; for if the skin of the child's head be cut while cutting the hair, it is known at once that some one has eat food. This is a sure sign. After the hair is cut the ceremony of *Poipoi* is again observed, and the *tohunga* then raising up his hands repeats this *karakia*, and the young person is free—

> These hands of mine are raised up,
> And this sacredness here.
> Tu-i-whiwhia, Tu-i-rawea,
> Your freedom from *tapu*
> Make sure the obtaining.
> Make sure the freedom.
> Make it sure to Papa.
> Give me my *tu* :
> Lift up the sacredness :
> Lift it up : it prevails.
> My hands here are raised[1] up,

---

[1] As to the custom of raising aloft the hands while praying to the Gods, compare Hom : Il. Lib. 3 273, and other numerous examples.

To Tiki there these hands of mine,
To Hine-nui-te-po these hands of mine,
These now free from *tapu*.
Freedom. They are free.

CEREMONIES FOR THE DEAD.

When a man dies his body is placed in a sitting posture, and is bound to a stake to keep it in a good position. It is seated with its face towards the sun as it rises from its cave. Then every one comes near to lament. The women in front, the men behind them. Their clothes are girded about their loins. In their hands they hold green leaves and boughs, then the song called *keka* commences thus :—

Tohunga chants		It is not a man,
All	„	{ It is Rangi now consigned to earth, { Alas! my friend.
Tohunga	„	My evil omen,
All	„	{ The lightning glancing on the mountain peak { Te Waharoa doomed to death.

After the *keka*, the *uhunga* or lament commences. The clothes in which the corpse should be dressed are the *kahuwaero*, the *huru*, the *topuni*, and the *tatata*. The lament ended, presents are spread to view, greenstone ornaments, and other offerings for the dead chief. A carved chest, ornamented with feathers, is also made, and a carved canoe, a small one resembling a large canoe, which is painted with *kokowai* (=red-ochre); also a stick bent at the top is set up by the way-side, in order that persons passing by may see it, and know that a chief has died. This is called a *hara*. The carved chest is called a *whare-rangi*. The corpse only is buried, the clothes are placed in the carved chest which is preserved by the family and descendants as a sacred relic.

On the morning following the burial, some men go to kill a small bird of the swamps called *kokata*, and to pluck up some reeds of *wiwi*. They return and come near the grave. The *tohunga* then asks "Whence come you?" The men reply, "From the seeking, from the searching." The *tohunga* again asks "Ah! what have you got? ah! what have you gained?" Thereon the men throw on the ground the *kotata* and the *wiwi*. Then the *tohunga* selects a stalk of *toetoe* or *rarauhe*, and places it near the grave in a direction pointing towards Hawaiki to be a pathway for the spirit, that it may go in the straight path to those who died before him. This is named a *Tiri*, and is also placed near where he died, in order that his spirit may return as an *Atua* for his living relations. The person to whom this *Atua* appears is called the *kaupapa* or *waka-atua*. Whenever the spirit appears to the *kaupapa* the men of the family assemble to hear its words. Hear the *karakia* of the *kaupapa* to prevail on the spirit to climb the path of the *Tiri*.

> This is your path, the path of Tawaki;
> By it he climbed up to Rangi,
> By it he mounted to your many,
> To your Thousands;
> By it you approached,
> By it you clung,
> By it your spirit arrived safely
> To your ancestors.
> I now am here sighing,
> Lamenting for your departed spirit,
> Come, come to me in form of a moth,
> Come to me your *kaupapa*,
> Whom you loved,
> For whom you lamented.
> Here is the *Tiri* for you,

The *Tiri* of your ancestors,
The *Tiri* of your *Pukenga*,
Of your *Wananga*,
Of me this *Tauira*.

THE REINGA OR HADES.

When the spirit leaves the body it goes on its way northward, till it arrives at two hills. The first of these hills is a place on which to lament with wailings and cuttings. There also the spirit strips off its clothes.[1] The name of this hill is Wai-hokimai. The name of the other hill is Wai-otioti: there the spirit turns its back on the land of life, and goes on to the Rerenga-wairua (Spirit's-leap). There are two long straight roots, the lower extremities of which are concealed in the sea, while the upper ends cling to a *pohutukawa* tree. The spirit stands by the upper end of these roots, awaiting an opening in the sea weed floating on the water. The moment an opening is seen, it flies down to the Reinga. Reaching the Reinga, there is a river and a sandy beach. The spirit crosses the river. The name of the new comer is shouted out. He is welcomed, and food is set before him. If he eats the food he can never return to life.[2]

TALE OF TE ATARAHI.

There was a man named Te Atarahi, who remained five nights and five days in the Reinga, and then returned to life. On the fifth day after this man died, two women went out to cut flax leaves. While so employed they

---

[1] Spirits on their way to the N. Cape are said to be clothed in the leaves of the *wharangi*, *makuku*, and *oropito*.

[2] Vid. similar account. "Traditions and Supersitions of the New Zealanders," p. 150, et seq.

observed the flower stalks of the flax springing up every now and then, at a little distance from them. Then one of the women remarked to her companion—" There is some one sucking the juice of the *korari* flowers." By degrees this person came nearer, and was seen by the woman, who said "the man is like Te Atarahi, why, it surely is Te Atarahi." Her companion replied—" It cannot be Te Atarahi, he is dead." Then they both looked carefully, and saw that the skin of the man was wrinkled and hanging loose about his back and shoulders, and that the hair of his head was all gone.

So the women returned to the *Pa*, and told how they had seen Te Atarahi. "Are you quite sure it was Te Atarahi?" said the men of the *Pa*. And the women answered, " His appearance was like Te Atarahi, but the hair of his head was all gone, and his skin hung loose in folds about his back." Then one was sent to look at the grave where Te Atarahi had been buried. He found the grave undisturbed, so he returned and said "Sirs, the body is well buried, it has not been disturbed." Then the men went, and examined the place carefully on every side, and found an opening on one side, a little way off. Then they went to the place where Te Atarahi had been seen by the women, and there found the man seated on a *ti* tree. They at once knew him to be Te Atarahi; so they sent for the *tohunga*. The *tohunga*, came and repeated a *karakia*, after which, the man was removed to the sacred place, and the *tohunga* remained with him constantly repeating *karakia*, while the people of the *Pa* stood without looking on. There the man remained many days, food being brought for him. Time passed, and he began to have again the appearance of a *Maori* man. At length he recovered and got quite well. Then he told how he had been in the Reigna, how his relations came about him, and bid him not to touch the food, and sent him back to the land of Light. He spoke also of the excellence of the state in which the people of the Reigna dwelt, of their food, of their choice delicacy the *ngaro*, of the numbers of their *Pa*, and the multitude of the dwellers there, all which agreed with what the *Atua* have said, when they visit men on earth.

NGA PATUPAIAREHE OR FAIRIES.

One day while Ruarangi was absent from his house a Patupaiarehe or Fairy came to it, and finding only the wife of Ruarangi within, carried her off to the hills. When the husband returned home his wife could not be found. He, however, traced footsteps to the hills where the Fairies dwelt, but saw nothing of his wife. Then he felt sure she had been carried off by the Fairies, and returned sorrowing and thinking of some plan to recover her. At length, having thought of a plan, he summoned the *tohunga* of the tribe—those skilled in bringing back love—those skilled in *makutu*—in short all the *tohunga*. When these all assembled before him, he said to them "The cause of my calling you is this. My wife has disappeared." The *tohunga* replied " When it is night, all of you leave your houses." So when night came every one came forth from his house as the *tohunga* had ordered. Then the *tohunga* skilled in restoring love stood up, and after some while discovered that the lost woman was with the Fairies. So he commenced a *karakia* to make her love for her *Maori* husband return.

> What wind is this blowing softly to your skin:
> Will you not incline towards your companion,

To whom you clung when sleeping together,
Whom you clasped in your arms,
Who shared your griefs.
When the wind bears to you this my love,
Incline hither thy love,
Sighing for the couch where both slept.
Let your love burst forth,
As the water-spring from its source.

When the *tohunga* had ended this *karakia* he said to
the husband "Go, fetch your wife. When she meets
you, be quick to rub her all over with *kokowai* (red-
ochre)." So the man went, and when night came he
lay down to sleep by the way side. While he slept he
saw his wife coming to meet him. With this he awoke
knowing well that the *tohunga* had spoken truly. At
day-light he went on his way, and after some time came
in sight of the *Pa* of the Fairies. No one was within
the *Pa*. All had gone forth to look at the *Maori*
woman. Now a great desire towards her *Maori* husband
had come to the woman borne to her by the *karakia* of
the *tohunga*, so the woman said to her Fairy husband
" Let me go and visit my new brothers-in-law." This
she said deceitfully ; for when her Fairy husband consented, she went straight away to meet her *Maori*
husband, who, as soon as she came near, rubbed her all
over with *kokowai*, and hastened home with her.

Meanwhile the Fairy husband awaited her return. He
waited a long while, and at last went to look for her: at
length he discovered footsteps of a man and woman,
then he knew she had gone off with her husband. So
the war-party of the Fairies assembled, and went to
attack the *Maori Pa*. But they found the posts of the
Pa daubed over with *kokowai*, and the leaves used in the

ovens for cooking, thrown on the roofs of the houses :
the *Pa* too was full of the steam of cooked food. As
for the woman, she was placed for concealment in an
oven.   So the Fairies feared to come near; for how could
they enter the *Pa* in their dread of the *kokowai*, and the
steam of the ovens which filled the court-yard. So great
is their dread of cooked food.

Then the *tohunga Maori* all standing up sung a *karakia*
to put to sleep the Fairies.

> Thrust aside, thrust afar,
> Thrust aside your sacredness,
> Thrust aside your *tohunga :*
> Let me, let me mark [1] you,
> Let me mark your brow,
> Give me thereupon your sacredness,
> You *mana*, your *tohunga*,
> Your *karakia* give me,
> To place beside the oven-stones,
> To place beside the cinders,
> To place beside the *kokowai*.
> Now these rest on your head,
> On your sacred places,
> On your female *Ariki*.
> Your sacredness is undone.

By the time this *karakia* came to an end, all the Fairies
were seated on the ground.   Their chief then stood up,
and sung thus :—

> Alas ! for this day
> Which now oppresses me.
> I stretched out my hand
> To the mate of Tirini.
> Followed were my footsteps,
> And charmed was returning love,

---

[1] With *kokowai*, or red-ochre.

E

At Pirongia there.
This the dreaded tribe is undone,
Tiki[1] and Nukupouri[1]
And Whanawhana[1]
And I Rangi-pouri:[1]
I carried off the woman,
I the first aggressor :
I went to enter the house of Ruarangi,
To stretch out my hand,
To touch the *Maori* skin.
The boundary is oven-marked,
To prevent its being moved aside,
To guard the wife in safety.

He thought the power of his *karakia* would appear ; but it could not conquer the devices of the *Maori tohunga* ; for how could it prevail against the cooked food, and the oven-stoves, and the *kokowai*, and the many other devices of the *tohunga*.   Hence it was seen that the power of *karakia* was not possessed by the Fairies.   The only power given to them was to smother men.

[1] Names of the Fairy chiefs.

CHAPTER V.

THE MAORI CHIEF OF OLDEN TIME.

Θεὸς δ'ὣς τίετο δήμῳ.—*Homer.*

THE Chiefs who came from Hawaiki to Aotea-roa in the canoe Arawa were the following:—Tia, Maka, Oro, Ngatoroirangi, Maru-punganui, Ika, Whaoa, Hei, and Tama-te-kapua. After their canoe was hauled ashore at Maketu, these chiefs set out to explore the country, in order to take possession of land each for himself and his family.

Tia and Maka went to Titiraupenga, at Taupo, and there remained.

Oro went to Taupo, and thence to Wanganui.

Ngatoroirangi went to Taupo, and died at Ruapehu.

Marupunga went to Rotorua, and died there.

Ika went to Wanganui, and died there.

Whaoa went to Paeroa.

Hei went to Whitianga (Mercury Bay). He was buried at O-a-Hei, on the extremity of the promontory.

Tama-te-kapua went to Moehau (Cape Colville).

Waitaha, son of Hei, and Tapuika, son of Tia, and Tangihia, son of Ngatoro-i-rangi, remained at Maketu. Tuhoro, and his younger brother, Kahumata-momoe, sons of Tama-te-kapua, also remained at Maketu. Their *Pa* was named Te Koari, and is still a sacred place. Their house was named Whitingakongako. Kahu had a cultivation named Parawai, which his mother gave him.

While he was at work one day in his garden, Tuhoro struck him, and they strove together. The elder brother fell, and being beneath his younger brother was held down by him on the ground. Then their children and the whole tribe cried out, "Let your elder brother rise up." So he let him go; but their quarrel continued with angry words. "Some day I will be the death of you," said Kahu, "and no one shall save you." Tuhoro, enraged, again struck Kahu; but he was thrown to the ground a second time by Kahu. Then Tuhoro seized hold of Kahu's ear, and tore from it a green-stone; the name of this stone was *kaukaumatua*. Tuhoro kept it, and some time afterwards buried it in the ground, at the foot of the post by the window of their father's house.

After this Tuhoro resolved to follow his father, Tama-te-kapua. So he went, he and all his children. He left none behind. He went to Moehau, and there he and his father both died.

When Tama-te-kapua was on the point of dying, he said to his son, Tuhoro, "You must remain sacred for three years, and dwell apart from the tribe. Let there be three gardens by the sides of your house, set apart as sacred, in which you are to cultivate food for the *Atua*. On the fourth year awaken me from sleep; for my hands will be ever gathering up the earth, and my mouth will be ever eating worms, and grubs, and excrement, the only food below in the *Reinga* (abode of spirits). When my *tuuta*[1] drops down, and my head falls down on my body, and my hands drop down, and the fourth year

[1] Point of junction of the spine and skull.

arrives, turn my face to the light of day, and disinter my *papa-toiake*.[1] When I arise you will be *noa* (free from *tapu*.)

> If clubs threaten to strike,
> You will see to it—Yes, yes.
> If a war party is abroad,
> You shall strike—Yes, yes."

Having thus said, Tama-te-kapua died, and was buried by his son on the summit of Moehau.

The three years enjoined by Tama were not ended, when Tuhoro commenced cultivating food as formerly ; so the sacred remains of his father turned against him, and he died.

A short time before his death, his sons, Taramainuku, Warenga, and Huarere, assembled in his presence. Whereupon Tuhoro said, "Your younger brother must bury me." So the younger son was called. Ihenga came and sat beside his father in his sacred house, who thus instructed him : "When I am dead, carry me out of the house, and lay me out naked to be your *Ika-hurihuri*[2] (twisting fish). First bite with your teeth my forehead, next bite with your teeth my *tahito*[3] (perineum). Then carry me to the grave of your grandfather. When I am buried, go to Maketu."

"Why must I go to Maketu ?"

"That your uncle may perform the ceremonies to remove your sacredness."

---

[1] Lower extremity of the spine..

[2] Omens were gathered from the movement of the dead body. The word fish or canoe is often used symbolically for a man.

[3] The perineum and head are considered the most sacred parts of the human body.

"But how shall I know him ?"

Then the father said, "He will not be unknown to you."

"Ho ! some one will kill me on the way."

"Not so. You will go in safety along the sea-shore."

"But I shall never find him."

"You cannot mistake him. Look at his right ear for a part hanging down. He is a big, short man, with a sleepy eye. When you approach your uncle, in order that he may know you, go at once and seat yourself on his pillow. When you are both freed from sacredness, search for the ear-drop of your uncle under the window-post."

"But how shall I find it ?"

"You will find it. Dig for it. It is buried there wrapt in a piece of cloth with *manuka* bark outside it."

So, when the father died, his naked body was brought out of the house, and laid on the ground. The younger son bit with his teeth the forehead, and then bit with his teeth the *tahito* of his father, saying at the same time, "Teach me when I sleep."

The reason why he bit the forehead and the *tahito* was that the *mana*, or sacred power of his father, might inspire him, so that he might become his *tauira*, *i.e.*, the living representative of his *mana* and *karakia*. Then the young man thus addressed the corpse : "If an enemy attack us hereafter, show me whether death or safety will be ours. If this land be abandoned, you and your father will be abandoned, and your offspring will perish."

Then the corpse moved, and inclined towards the

right side. Afterwards it inclined towards the left side. A second time it inclined to the right, and afterwards to the left side. After that the moving of the body ceased. Therefore it was seen that it was an ill-omen, and that the land would be deserted.

After this laying out of the corpse, its legs were bent, so that the knees touched the neck, and then it was bound in this position with a plaited girdle. Afterwards two cloaks, made of *kahakaha*, were wrapt around the corpse, over which were placed two cloaks such as old men wear, and then a dog-skin cloak. Feathers of the albatross, the *huia*, and the *kotuku* (white crane), were stuck in the hair of the head, and the down breasts of the albatross were fastened to the ears. Then commenced the *tangi* (dirge, or lament). Then the last farewell words were spoken, and the chiefs made speeches. The lament of Rikiriki, and the lament of Raukatauri for Tuhuruhuru was chanted; and the corpse was buried on the ridge of Moehau.

Now, when the young man slept, the spirit of his father said to him, "When you are hungry, do not allow your mouth to ask for food; but strike with a stick the food-basket. If you are thirsty, strike the gourd." Every night the spirit of the father taught the young man his *karakia*, till he had learnt them all ; after which he said to his son, " Now we two will go, and also some one to carry food."

So they went both of them, the father's spirit leading the way. Starting from Moehau they passed by Heretaonga, Whangapoua, Tairua, Whangamata, Katikati, and Matakana. There they rested. After that they went on to Rangiwaea, where Ihenga embarked in a small sacred canoe, while his travelling companion went on board a large canoe. Then they crossed over to Waikoriri. Here Waitara wished to detain him, but he would not stay. He went straight onwards to Wairakei, and the Houhou. He met a man, and enquired where Kahu dwelt. The man said, " At the great house you see yonder." So Ihenga went on, and having reached the place where the Arawa was hauled ashore, he looked about him, and then went on to the sacred place, the Koari, and there left his father's *ueta*[1]. He then ascended the cliff to the Teko, and climbing over Kahu's doorway, went straight on to the sacred part of the courtyard, and seated himself on Kahu's pillow.

Meanwhile Kahu was on the beach, where guests were usually entertained, busied about sending off a canoe with food for the *Atua* at Hawaiki, and for Houmaitahiti, food both cooked and uncooked. This canoe was made of *raupo* (a species of bulrush). There was no one in the canoe, only stones to represent men. There Kahu was busied sending off his canoe, when his wife, Kuiwai, shouted to him, " Kahu, Kahu, there is a man on your resting place." Then Kahu cried out, " Take him ; shove him down here." The woman replied, " Who will dare to approach your pillow ; the man is *tapu*." Then Kahu shouted, " Is he seated on my pillow ?" " Yes." " I am mad with anger," said Kahu ; " his head shall pay for it."

Ihenga was dressed in two dog-skin cloaks, under

---

[1] The *ueta* is a whisp of weeds or grass used to wipe the anus of the corpse. It is afterwards bound to a stick, and is carried as a talisman.

which were two *kahakaha* cloaks. As Kahu went up
towards the *Pa* he asked, " Which way did the man
come." The woman replied, " He climbed over your
gate."

By this time Kahu had reached the fence, and caught
sight of the young man.

He no sooner saw him than he recognised his likeness
to his brother, Tuhoro, and straightway welcomed him
—" Oh ! It is my nephew. Welcome, my child, welcome." He then began lamenting, and murmuring
words of affection over him ; so the tribe knew that it
was the young son of Tuhoro.

After the lament, Kahu made inquiry for his brother,
and the young man said, " My father is dead. I buried
him. I have come to you to perform the ceremonies of
the *pure* and the *horohoro*, to remove my sacredness."
Immediately Kahu shouted to the tribe, "The *marae*
(courtyard) is *tapu*," and led the young man to the sacred
house of the priests. He then ordered food to be
prepared—a dog of the breed of Irawaru—and while it
was being cooked, went with the young man to dip
themselves in the river. His companion, a son of his
brother, Warenga, remained with the rest of the tribe.
When they had dipped in the river, Kahu commenced
cutting the young man's hair, which is a part of the
ceremony of *Pure*. In the evening, the hair being cut,
the *mauri*,[1] or sacredness of the hair, was fastened to a
stone.

---

[1] The hair of the head, in this ceremony, was made fast to a stone,
   and the sacredness of the hair was supposed to be transferred to
   this stone, which represented some ancestor. The stone and hair
   were then carried to the sacred place belonging to the *Pa*.

Then Kahu went with Ihenga to the Koari, where the *ueta* of the corpse had been left, and there chanted a *karakia*. They then rested for the night.

The next morning the ceremony of the *Pure* was finished, and the following *karakia* was chanted by Kahu :—

> Complete the rite of Pure,
> By which you will be free from
> The evil influence of Po,
> The bewitching power of Po.
> Free the canoe from sacredness, O Rangi ;
> The canoe of stumbling unawares, O Rangi ;
> The canoe of death unawares, O Rangi.
> Darkness for the Tipua, darkness.
> Darkness for the Antient-one, darkness.
> Some light above,
> Some light below.
> Light for the Tipua, light.
> Light for the Antient-one, light.
> The *uwha*[1] is held aloft.
> A squeeze, a squeeze.
> Protection from Tu.

After this they went to partake of food ; and the oven of the *kohukohu*[2] was opened. While the oven was being uncovered by Hine-te-kakara (the fragrant damsel), she took care to turn aside her face, lest the savour of the *kumara* and the steam of the sacred oven should come near her mouth, lest evil should come to her. She did not even swallow her spittle, but constantly kept spitting it forth.

---

[1] *Uwha*, the bivalve shell used for cutting the hair.

[2] *Kohukohu*, the plant chick-weed, in the leaves of which the sacred *kumara* was wrapped.

When the food was set before Kahu and Ihenga, Ihenga took up some of the *kohukohu* in which were wrapt two *kumara*, and held it in his hand, while Kahu chanted the following *karakia* :—

> Rangi, great Rangi,
> Long Rangi, dark Rangi,
> Darkling Rangi, white-star Rangi,
> Rangi shrouded in night.
> Tane the first, Tane the second,
> Tane the third, &c.
> (Repeated to Tane the tenth).
> Tiki, Tiki of the mound of earth,
> Tiki gathered in the hands,
> To form hands and legs,
> And the fashion of a man,
> Whence came living men.
> Toi,
> Rauru,
> Whetima,
> Whetango,
> Te Atua-hae,
> Toi-te-huatahi,
> Tuamatua,
> Houmaitahiti,
> Ngatoroirangi,
> And your first born male
> Now living in the light of day.

While Kahu chanted thus, the *kohukohu* was held in the hand of Ihenga. Kahu then proceeded with the direct male line—

> Tangihia,
> Tangimoana,
> Tumakoka,
> Tukahukura,
> Tuhoto,
> Tarawhai.

There ended the recitation of Kahu, and he went on to his own proper line—

> Houmaitahiti,
> Tama,
> Tuhoro,
> And to your offspring born to life,
> And to the light of day.
> This is your *kohukohu* of the *horohoronga*,
> To make light the weight of *tapu*.
> He is free, he is released from *tapu*.
> He goes safely where food is cooked,
> To the evil mighty spirits of Night,
> To the kind mighty spirits of Night,
> To the evil mighty spirits of Light,
> To the kind mighty spirits of Light.

Then the *kohukohu* was offered as food to the stone images, and was divided for Houmaitahiti, for Ngatoroirangi, for Tama-te-kapua, and for Tuhoro, and was pressed into their mouths[1]. This being done Ihenga took up another *kohukohu*, and held it in his hand raising it aloft, while Kahu chanted the following *karakia* :—

> For Hine-nui-te-po,
> For Whati-uri-mata-kaka,
> For the evil old women of Night,
> For the kind old women of Night,
> For the evil old women of Day,
> For the kind old women of Day,
> For Kearoa,
> Whose offspring is born to life,

---

[1] Hence the term *horohoronga* (=swallowing) given to the ceremony. It is to be remarked that the distinguishing name given to various ceremonies was taken from some striking circumstances connected with it,—thus, a sacred oven is named *kohukohu* from the leaves of the plant in which the *kumara* was wrapt : &c.

And to the bright light of day,
This *kohukohu* is offered for you,
The *kohukoku* of the *Ruahine*.
He is free, he is no longer *tapu*.

The female *Atua* were then fed with the *kohukohu* as in the former case.   Then part of the *kohukohu* was offered for the mother, Whaka-oti-rangi.[1]

Turn away Night,
Come Day.
This is the *kohukohu* of freedom,
And deliverance from *tapu*.

This done, Ihenga took up another *kohukohu*, and held it aloft in his hand, while Kahu chanted thus :—

Close up Night, close up Day,
Close up Night as the soft south wind.
The *tapu* of the food
And the *mana* of the food,
The food with which you are fed,
The food of Kutikuti,
The food of Pekapeka,
The food of Haua-te-rangi.
I eat, Uenuku eats.
I eat, Kahukura eats.
I eat, Rongomai eats.
I eat, Ihungaro eats.
I eat, Itupaoa eats.
I eat, Hangaroa eats.
I eat, Ngatoro-irangi eats.
I eat, Tama eats.

[1] Kearoa and Whaka-oti-rangi being both sacred female ancestors—wives of Ngatoro and Tama, represented the *Ruahine*, the swallowing of this food by whom was requisite in removing the *tapu*. The *tapu*, or sacredness of Kahu, was supposed to be transferred to the *kohukohu*, and when this was eat by the ancestral spirits, the *tapu* was deposited with them.

This ended, Kahu proceeded thus :

    If I fall from the precipice,
    Let me not be harmed.
    If I fall on the *taramoa*,
    Let me not be scratched.
    If I eat of the *maihi*[1] of *tohunga's* house,
    Let me not be harmed.
    Be thou undermost,
    While I am uppermost.
    Give me your *mana* to strike down.
    Close tight your spirit-devouring teeth.
    Close tight your man-devouring teeth.

Then Kahu spat on the *kohukohu*, breathed on it, and offered it to Tama, that is to say, to the image of Tama-te-kapua. Kahu and Ihenga then ate the food cooked for them in the sacred oven. Ihenga ate with a fork, while at the same time he fed Kahu with his left hand.

The same ceremonies were observed at the evening meal.

Eight days after the ceremony of *Pure*, the heart of Ihenga conceived a desire. He was taken with the fair face of Hinetekakara; so he asked Kahu, "When shall we two be free from *tapu* ?" Kahu replied "We two will not soon be free." "Oh! be quick," said Ihenga, "that I may return to my elder brothers, to my mother, and to my sisters." Kahu said, "You will not be dismissed soon—not until the *tapu* is completely removed from you." "How many nights, then, after this ?"

---

[1] *Maihi* are the two boards placed at an angle at front gable of a house. If the wood of a sacred house were to be accidentally used as firewood for cooking purposes, anyone who ate the food thus cooked would be guilty of a crime, to be punished by the *Atua* with disease or death.

Kahu answered, "Twenty nights."

"Ho! what a very long time," said Ihenga, "for our *tapu*."

The remonstrance of the young man here ended; but not long afterwards he persisted in the same manner. Thereupon Kahu began to consider—"Ha! what is it my nephew persists about?" So he asked, "Why are you in so great a hurry to be free from *tapu*?" Then the young man spoke out, "Whose daughter is the maiden who cooks our food?"

"Mine," replied Kahu.

"My fear," said Ihenga, "lest some one may have her."

"I thought there must be something."

"Do not let some other man have her."

"Your cousin shall be your wife," said Kahu, calling the damsel: "Come here, girl, near the door."

The girl came laughing, for she knew she was to be given to Ihenga.

Then said Kahu: "Your cousin has a longing for you."

"It is well," replied the damsel.

"Oh! my children," murmured Kahu. He then cautioned his daughter not to enter the house where young people resort for amusement.

"I never go to the play-house," replied Hinetekakara, "I always sleep with my mother in our own house,"

"You do well," said Kahu;" "in twenty days we shall both be free from our *tapu*."

So they both continued to dwell in their sacred house by themselves, and the damsel always cooked food for

them; and when the day fixed by Kahu came he sent
Ihenga in a canoe to catch fish to complete the ceremony of removing the *tapu*. The fish were caught,
and two ovens were prepared to cook them — a
sacred oven for the *tohunga*, or seers skilled in sacred
lore—and a free oven for the *tauira*, or those being instructed in sacred lore. And when the food was cooked they
assembled to eat it : the *tohunga* on the right hand fed each
other by hand, and the *tauira* on the left ate freely their
unsacred food. This was done to lighten the weight of
the *tapu*, in order that they might be free. When all
this was done, and they were no longer *tapu*, Hinetekakara became the wife of Ihenga.

The following morning Ihenga searched for the green-
stone *kaukaumatua*, and found it in the place where
Tuhoro had buried it. He then fastened it to the ear
of Hinetekakara, bidding her go and show the treasure
to her father. When Kahu beheld his lost treasure
hanging from his daughter's ear he gave utterance to his
feelings with tears and words of affection for his dead
brother, and when the *tangi* or lament was ended, bid
her keep the treasure for herself, and for her cousin.

Some time afterwards Hinetekakara conceived, and
Ihenga went to catch *kiwi* for her *turakanga*.[1] He took
with him his dog Potakatahiti, one of the same breed as
the dog of the same name which was devoured by Toi
and Uenuku.[2] Crossing the swamp Kawa, he went to

---

[1] *Turakanga* (=throwing down) was a ceremony in which a stick set
up to represent the path of death was thrown down. A form of
karakia was, at the same time, used.

[2] Vid : Sir G. Grey's "Mythology and Traditions," p. 63.

Papanui, and arriving at the cross-road at Waipumuka ascended the hill Paretawa. Thence he went on to Hakomiti, and Pukerangiora, and began to hunt *kiwi*. The dog feeling the heat, and becoming thirsty, went off in search of water, at the same time hunting *kiwi*. When he caught a *kiwi* he left it on the ground. At last a *kiwi* ran a long way, and tried to escape by running into a lake where the dog caught it. The dog then began to catch in its mouth the small fish called *inanga ;* and having filled its belly returned by the way it had come, always picking up the *kiwi*, which it had left on the ground, and carrying them in his mouth, till he reached his master, laid them on the ground before him. Seeing the dog dripping with water, Ihenga said to his companions, "Ho! the dog has found water. There is a lake below, perhaps." However they did not then go to look for it, for they were busied about cooking food. Meanwhile the dog began to roll on the ground in front of Ihenga, belly upwards. It then lay down, but not long after began to vomit, and the *inanga* were seen lying on the ground. Then they went to look for the water, and the dog ran before them barking every now and then to let his master know which way he was going. In this way they soon came to the lake. Shoals of *inanga* were leaping on the water; so they made a net with branches of fern, and having caught a great many, cooked some for food; after which they returned to Maketu, carrying with them basketsful of *inanga* to show to Kahu, that he might know how the lake abounded with food. Ihenga named the lake "Te Roto-iti-kite-a-Ihenga (=the small lake discovered by Ihenga), thus claiming it as a possession for his children.

F

When they reached Maketu Ihenga told Kahu about the lake he had discovered.

" Where is it ?" inquired Kahu.

" Beyond the hills."

" Is it a long way off?"

" Yes," said Ihenga.

" Beyond the first range of hills ?" inquired Kahu.

" At the sixth range of hills," said Ihenga.

" Oh ! it is near," said Kahu.

Then Ihenga bid his companions show Kahu the food they had brought.

But Kahu said, " No ; leave it alone till to-morrow."

The next morning the oven was made ready for the ceremony of *Turakanga*. Hinetekakara dipped in the river, and two mounds of earth were made—one for a male child, and one for a female child. The path of death was thrown down, and the path of life set up. Then the woman trampled on the mound for the male child with one foot, and with the other foot she trampled on the mound for the female child. Then she ran and plunged in the river, and when she rose to the surface she swam ashore, put on her *tawaru*, and returned to her house.

When the food was cooked all the men assembled to eat it—the men of the race of Houmaitahiti. There were six hundred *kiwi*, and two baskets of *inanga*. And as he was eating Kahu murmured, " Ho ! ho ! what prime food for my grandchild."

After some time a child was born and was named Tama-ihu-toroa, and when it grew strong in limb, so that it could turn about from one side to the other, Kahu said to Ihenga, " Go, seek lands for your child."

CHAPTER VI.

CLAIMING AND NAMING LAND.

No place in the world ever received a name which could not
be accounted for, though there are hundreds of such names
of which we can now give no explanation.—*Farrar on
Language*, p. 22.

IHENGA set out with four companions.   He went in a
different direction to that of his former journey.   He
now went by way of Mataparu, Te Hiapo, Te Whare-
pakau-awe.   When on the summit of the ridge he
looked back towards Maketu, and greeted his home
there.   Then turning round he saw the steam of the
hot springs at Ruahine.   Believing it to be smoke from
a fire, he said to his companions, "Ha! that land has
been taken possession of by some one.   Let us go on."
They entered the forest, and having passed through it,
came to a waterfall.   Afterwards they came to a lake in
which was a large island.   Proceeding along the shore
of the lake Ihenga gave names to various places.   On
arriving at a point of land jutting out into the lake,
which he named Tuara-hiwi-roa, they halted; for they
saw a flock of shags perched on the stumps of some
trees in the lake.   They made snares and fastened them
to a pole to catch the shags, and placed the pole on the
stumps of the trees.   Presently the shags perched on
the pole, and were caught in the snares, some by the legs
and some by the neck.   But the shags flew off with the
snares, pole and all.   The young men thought they
would alight in the lake, but Ihenga said, "No, they
are flying on; they will alight on Te Motu-tapu-a-

Tinirau." Ihenga had given this name to the island, which was afterwards named Mokoia by Uenuku-kopako.

Then Ihenga went alone in pursuit of his birds along the borders of the lake. He passed by Ohinemutu, where he found the hot springs, and the steam which he had supposed to be the smoke of a fire. When he reached the hill at Kawaha, looking down he saw the smoke of a fire burning below at Waiohiro; so he thought with himself, "Shall I go on, or no?" He decided on the no; for he saw a net hanging near a stage, on which there was food, so he went to look for the *tuahu* or sacred place for the net. When he had found it he forthwith set to work to carry off the earth, and the posts, and the old decaying *inanga,* in order to make a *tuahu* for himself by the face of the cliff at Kawaha. Then he brought fresh earth and new posts to the *tuahu* of the man of the place, and carried away some posts partly burnt by fire. He also stript off the bark from branches of *koromuka* and *angiangi,* and fastened them together with flax, and set them up in the inclosure of the *tuahu* belonging to the man of the place. When Ihenga had done all this secretly, he named his own *tuahu* Te Pera-o-tangaroa, and went on to the place where the fire was burning.

As soon as he was seen, the people of the place waved their cloaks, and shouted cries of welcome. And when the ceremony of *uhunga* was ended, the chief, whose name was Tu-o rotorua, inquired when Ihenga had come to the lake.

" Ho! this is my own land," said Ihenga.

" Where is your land ?" asked Tu.

"Why, this very land," replied Ihenga. "I ought rather to ask you how long you have been here ?"

"Why, I have been here this long time."

"No, no! I was here first."

"No," said Tu, "I and your uncle were first here."

Ihenga, however, persisted. "Ho! surely you came last. The land belongs to me."

"What sign have you," said Tu, "to shew that the land is yours ?"

"What is your sign ?" replied Ihenga.

"A *tuahu*," said Tu.

"Come on," said Ihenga, "let me see your *tuahu*. If your *tuahu* is older than mine, you truly came first, and the land is yours."

Tu consented, and led the way to his *tuahu*. When they arrived there, it had the appearance of having been newly made.

Then said Ihenga, "Now come and look at my *tuahu*, and my *ngakoa*.[1] So they went together to the Pera-o-tangaroa, where they found a heap of decaying and dried old *inanga* which Ihenga had brought there from the *tuahu* of Tu-o-rotorua. So when Tu beheld them, and the old burnt posts which Ihenga had stolen, he was so puzzled that he was almost persuaded that Ihenga must have been the first to occupy the land. However, he said, "let me see your net."

"Come up higher," said Ihenga, "and I will shew you

[1] *Ngakoa* were offerings to the *Atua* of fish and other kinds of food.

my net." And he then pointed to a mark on a distant cliff, caused by a landslip.

"Why, that is a landslip," said Tu.

"No," said Ihenga, "it is a net quite new. Look at that other net which is hanging up, and looks black; that is the old net."

Tu thought it must be as Ihenga said, so he agreed to leave the land, asking at the same time who lived on the island.

"The name of the island, said Ihenga, "is Motu-tapu-a-Tinirau. I named it."

Then said Tu, "Will you not consent to my living there?"

"Yes," said Ihenga, "you may go to the island." Thus the main land came to the possession of Ihenga.

Then Ihenga borrowed a small canoe belonging to Tu, and went on in search of his flock of shags. He found them hanging in a *kahikatea* tree near Waikuta. He called the stream by that name because of the plant *kuta*, which grew abundantly there. He named the land Ra-roa, because of the length of the day occupied in his canoe. He climbed the tree and threw down the birds, and placed them in the canoe. Then he went on and came to a river which he afterwards named Ngongo-taha. There was a hill hard by to which he gave the same name. The hill belonged to the Patupaiarehe or Fairies. They had a *Pa* on the hill named Tuahu-o-te-atua. He heard them playing on the *putorino*,[1] the *koauau*,[1] and the *putara*;[1] so he thought men must be

---

[1] Different kinds of wind instruments resembling the flute, only varying in their length.

living there. He climbed the hill, and when he got
near, he heard the sounds of the *haka* and *waiata* :—

> A canoe, a canoe,
> A canoe of flax, a canoe.
> Grow *kawa*,
> Blaze *kawa*.
> Tie up carefully
> With leaf of flax,
> Blazing *kawa*.

Whakatauihi made this *haka*. His was also the proverb, " *ko te ure tonu* ; *ko te raho tonu*." He it was who
avenged the death of Tuhuruhuru.[1]

When Ihenga got nearer he perceived that they were
not men, but *Atua*. There was a fire burning on a tree.
So he stopt suddenly to look at them, while they looked
at him. "A *nanakia*," shouted one of them, running
forward to catch him. But Ihenga fled, and, as he was
running, set fire to the dry fern with a lighted brand he
had in his hand. The whole fern was ablaze, and the
tribe of Fairies fled to the forest and the hills. Then
Ihenga went back to look at their *Pa* which had been
burnt by the fire. There he found the *kauae* or jaw-bone
of a *moa*, so he named the place Kauae. He then
returned to the shore of the lake, and went on in his
canoe. He named the hill Ngongotaha, because of the
flight of the Fairies.

Ihenga paddled along the shores of the lake
giving names to many places as he went—Weriweri,
Kopu, Te Awahou, Puhirua—which last he so named
because the bunch of feathers fastened to his *paiaka* fell
off. At another place the *inanga* leaped out of the

---

[1] Vide "Traditions and Superstitions," p. 68.

water, and some fell into his canoe, so he named it
Tane-whiti. Another place he named from a boastful
thought in his mind, Tu-pakaria-a-Ihenga (Ihenga's
boasting). He passed by the river Ohau. He had
named this river before, when he first came to the lake,
from the name of his dog. As the dog was swimming
across it was drawn in by a whirlpool, and so was
drowned. Next he came to the land-slip on the mountain which he had made Tu believe to be a net. He
named it Te Tawa, because he left there a pole used for
pushing the canoe, which was made of the wood *tawa*.
The pole stuck so fast in the ground that he could not
pull it out, so he left it there. After passing the point
Tuara-hiwi-roa he came in sight of his companions.
The shout resounds, " Oh ! it is Ihenga. Come here,
come here, sir—paddle hither." His wife ran down to
the water side as the canoe touched the beach.

" See what food you have lying there," said Ihenga.
Hine-te-kakara caught up a bundle of rats, and when
she saw their teeth she exclaimed " ē, ē, *he niho kiore*"
(eh ! eh ! a rat's tooth). So the place was named Te
Niho-o-te-kiore. Again she made an exclamation of
admiration at the heap of birds, " In truth, in truth, a
wonderful heap. Come, sirs, come and look at it." So
that place was also named " Kahui-kawau," or Flock of
Shags. Then the birds were cooked, and the next day
they all departed to return to Maketu. They went to
fetch Kahu. The food, the shags, the bundle of rats,
the gourd of *inanga*, and the gourd of *porohi*[1]—a
tempting bait to make Kahu come.

[1] *Porohi*, a small fish of the lake.

They reached the Hiapo, and rested there the night. Kuiwai and Haungaroa gave that name, because they left their brother Hiapo there, and he died there. Hiapo saw the *koko* hopping about the trees, and remained behind while his sisters went on to Maketu to carry messages from Hawaiki to Ngatoroirangi.

The next day they went on, and when they reached Totara-keria they were seen from the *Pa* by Tawaki. Then came shouts from the *Pa*, "Come, heaven-sent guest, brought hither by my child from beyond the sky. Come, come." They arrive—the *tangi* commences—then speeches are made. Meanwhile food is being prepared. When they had done eating the food, Tawaki said to Ihenga, "Tell us about your travels. Whence come you, lost one?"

"I have seen a sea," said Ihenga, "I found a man there."

"Who is the man?" asked Tawaki.

"Marupunga-nui, and his son."

They all knew that the son was Tu-o-rotorua. So Kahu inquired "Where is your uncle and his father?"

"They remain there," said Ihenga, "I have made them go to the island."

"Well done, son-in-law," said Kahu.

Then the food brought by the men was laid in a pile before Tawaki in the courtyard of Whitingakongako. And Tawaki said to his sister "Give some for me and your father." So she gave the bundle of rats, and the shags, and the gourd of *inanga*, and the other fish. And Tawaki and his father sent them to their own dwelling-place.

As he was eating the food Kahu exclaimed " Ha! ha! food sent from the sky, food of Aotea-roa. Why that land of yours is Hawaiki. Food falling into your mouth."

"Yes, yes," said Ihenga, "first kindle the oven. When it is heated you fetch the food from that sea in baskets full."

Then said Kahu "Ah! that land is a land for you, and for your wife, and for your offspring."

"Let us all go there," said Ihenga. To which Kahu consented.

Then Ihenga said, " Let the *mana* of that land go to you. You are the *Ariki* of that land—you and your offspring."

"Yes," replied Kahu. " Since you, my *Ariki*, are so great a gentleman as to bid the younger brother's son dwell on that land of yours. Yes—I consent that we all go."

Then the food brought by Hinetekakara was portioned among the whole tribe.

Ten days afterwards they left Maketu, twenty in number, ten of the rank of chiefs, and ten men to carry food. When they reached the small lake, discovered by Ihenga, he said to Kahu "You are the *Ariki* of this lake." Hence the song of Taipari—

> By Hakomiti was your path hither
> To Pariparitetai, and to that Rotoiti of yours,
> Sea discovered by Ihenga,
> Thereof Kahu was *Ariki*.

Thence they went on to Ohou-kaka, so named by Kahu from a parrot-feather *hou-kaka*, which he took

from the hair of his head, and stuck in the ground to
become a *taniwha* or spirit monster for that place.
When they reached the place where their canoes had
been left they launched two, a small sacred canoe for
Kahu, and a large canoe for the others. Then they
embarked, and as they paddled along coming near a
certain beach, Kahu threw off his clothes, and leaped
ashore, naked. His two grandsons, Tama-ihu-toroa and
Uenuku, laughed and shouted "Ho! ho! see, there go
Kahu's legs." So the place was named Kuwha-rua-o-
Kahu. In this way they proceeded, giving names to
places not before named, till they reached Lake Rotorua.
They landed at Tuara-hiwi-roa, and remained there
several nights, and built a *whata*, or food-store raised on
posts; so that place was named Te Whata.

Then going on by way of the Hot Springs, they
arrived at Te Pera-o-tangaroa, and Wai-o-hiro, the
stream where Tu-o-rotorua formerly dwelt. Next they
came to Ngongotaha, which Kahu named Parawai, after
his garden at Maketu.

After they had dwelt two whole years at Parawai Kahu
determined to visit his nephew Taramainuku. Taramainuku and Warenga, the elder brothers of Ihenga, had
abandoned the land at Moehau. The former had gone
to the Wairoa at Kaipara, and the latter to the Kawakawa
at the Bay of Islands, and had settled there. So Kahu
set out with his son-in-law Ihenga, and his son Tawaki,
and some travelling companions. He left behind at
Parawai his daughter Hine-te-kakara, and her son
Tama-ihu-toroa. He also left Uenuku, the son of
Tawaki, and his wife, Waka-oti-rangi, to keep possession
of Parawai as a permanent abode for them.

Arriving at the hills they rested, and Kahu sought a shelter under a *rata* tree, which he named Te Whaka-marumaru-o-Kahu (Kahu's shelter). Thereupon Ihenga perceiving that Kahu was giving his own name to the land, pointed to a *matai* tree; for he saw a root jutting out from the trunk of the tree resembling a man's thigh; he therefore named it Te Ure-o-Tuhoro. He named it after his father's *ure* to weigh down the name of Kahu, his father-in-law, so that the place might go to his own descendants. And it went to his descendants, and is now in possession of Ngatitama. As they went on Kahu's dog caught a *kakapo*, so he named the place Te Kakapo. A little further on they came to a part of the hill where a stone projected from the face of the cliff. Then Kahu chanted a *karakia* called *Uru-uru-whenua* :—

> I come to Matanuku,
> I come to Matarangi,
> I come to your land,
> A stranger.
> Feed thou on the heart of the stranger.
> Put to sleep mighty spirits,
> Put to sleep ancient spirits,
> Feed thou on the heart of the stranger.

So he named the place Matanuku, which name remains to this day.

Arriving on the banks of the river Waikato he crossed over and rested while food was being cooked. The young men were very dilatory, and Kahu was angry at their laziness; so he named the place Mangare. Afterwards they came to the river Waipa, crossing which they passed over Pirongia to Waingaroa, and thence along the sea beach to the mouth of the river Waikato. Here they fell in with Ohomairangi. He came in Tainui. He was the brother of Tuikakapa, a wife of Houmaitahiti, and mother of Tama-te-kapua and Whakaturia.

From Waikato they proceeded along the sea beach to Manuka, so named by Kahu who set up a *manuka* post there as a *rahui* or sacred mark. Here Kahu's companions embarked in a canoe, while he prevailed on a *taniwha* or sea monster of that place, named Paikea, to carry him on his back. At length they drew near to Kaipara, and falling in with some of the men of Taramainuku were conveyed by them in their canoes to Pouto, where Tara was residing on the banks of the river Wairoa.

The *tangi* resounded, and speeches of welcome followed—"Come here, come here, my father. Come to visit us, and to look on us. I have deserted your elder brother and your father" (meaning their bodies left buried at Moehau).

Then Kahu spoke—"Welcome us, welcome us, my *Ariki*. Behold us here. I the suffering one come to you. I thought that you, my *Ariki*, would seek me. But it is well, for I now behold you face to face, and you also behold me. I and your younger brother will return to our own place, that I may die on the land which your grandfather[1] in his farewell words to me and my elder brother named as a land for you. I was deserted by my elder brother on account of our strife about the garden. But that land is not for the younger brother only—no, it is for all of you alike. But I will not part with your

---

[1] Tama-te-kapua.

younger brother, and for this reason I gave him your cousin for wife."

"It is well," said Taramainuku; "has not your son, Tawaki, a child?"

"Yes, Uenuku."

"Then carry home with you his cousin to be his wife."

To this Kahu consented. So Taramainuku's daughter, Hine-tu-te-rauniao, was given to Kahu to return with him to Rotorua. The son of Uenuku and Hine was Rangitiki.

Then Taramainuku's wife placed food before the guests, *toheroa*[1], eels, *hinau*[2], *kumara, hue*[3], and a basket of *para*.[4]

When Kahu saw the *para*, he asked, "What food is this?"

"It is *para*," replied his nephew.

"And where does it grow?" asked Kahu.

"It grows in the woods."

"Ho!" said Kahu, "this is the food your ancestor ate. It is the *raho* of your ancestor, Tangaroa. This is the first time I have tasted *para*. You must call this place Kaipara."

Kahu returned homewards from Kaipara, but Ihenga stayed with his elder brother. Kahu returned by way of Waitemata, embarking in a canoe at Takapunga. He

---

[1] *Toheroa*, a species of bivalve.
[2] *Hinau*, berry of Elœocarpus dentatus.
[3] *Hue*, a small gourd.
[4] *Para*, a species of fern having a tuberous root.

passed by Motu-ihe, and Paritu on the north of Waiheke,
and crossed over to Moehau.   There he found Huarere
and his family.   The *tangi* being ended, speeches were
made.   Meanwhile food was prepared ; and when they
had finished eating the food, Huarere said, " Your *papa*
(uncle) has been here."

" Who ?" inquired Kahu.

" Ngatoro-i-rangi."

" Ho ! where is he ?"

" He has gone away," replied Huarere.   " He came
in search of you.   He set up a stone for a token for
you."

" ē, ē, my *papa*, ē, ē," murmured Kahu.

Huarere continued : " After the arrival of your *papa*
he went directly to disinter the bones of Tama and
Tuhoro."

" That is well," said Kahu.

Having remained three nights Kahu and his companions, with Huarere, climbed to the summit of the
mountain where Tama-te-kapua had been laid to sleep.
Therefore the mountain was named Moe-hau-o-Tama,
or Sleeping Sacredness of Tama.   After three nights
Kahu went on to the forest, and set up a *Ri*, or sacred
mark, as a warning to prevent anyone from passing
further that way.   It remains there to this day.   Then
descending to the beach he turned his face towards the
mountain, and chanted a lament to the resting place of his
elder brother; so that place was named Tangi-aro-o-Kahu.
He then went to see the stone which Ngatoro had set
up as a token for him.   That place is named Te Kohatu-

whakairi-a-Ngatoro, and the stone remains there to this day. Then he climbed another hill, and placed a stone on its summit. The stone was named Tokatea. Thence they travelled along the ridge of the hills till they reached a lofty peak. They ascended it, and remained seated there, while Kahu looked about on every side. "Ho! ho!" said Kahu, "this is an island," and turning to Huarere, "your land, my child."

They went along the ridge of the hills that they might see the goodness of the land. The goodness of the land was seen, and Kahu said to his nephew, "The goodness of the land is this; there are two flood tides. The east tide flows while the west tide is ebbing." Then they descended to the water side, where they saw fish called *auz*,[1] so they named the water Wai-aua.

Kahu and Huarere then parted. The descendants of Huarere grew and multiplied there, and all those lands became filled with them.

Kahu went on his way to Rotorua, and after several days reached the place where the river Waihou divides into two branches. There he rested, and when he felt the soft sea-breeze over the rippling tide, words of affection came from his lips; so the place was named Muri-aroha-o-Kahu (the regret of Kahu). On they went, and climbing a lofty mountain Kahu looked towards the sea, and thus gave vent to his affection: "Ah! my love to Moehau, alas for the land of my father, and of my elder brother, far away over the sea." So that mountain was named Aroha-tai-o-Kahu. Then Kahu turned his face landward, and murmured words of affection toward

---

[1] *Aua*, a fish resembling the herring.

the land at Titiraupenga, to Tia and Maka. Hence the
name of the other mountain, Aroha-o-uta-o-Kahu. They
then travelled along the mountain ridge which he named
Tau-o-hanga. This name belongs to the whole mountain ridge from Moehau as far as the Wairoa.

At length they entered the forest which extends
towards Rotorua. Rain fell, and they were drenched
with water dripping from the trees. Then Kahu chanted
an invocation to Rangi, and the rain ceased. Kahu
named the place Patere-o-Kahu, from their having been
drenched with the rain. At the birth of the son of
Hopo, the child was named Patetere.

At length they passed through the forest, and arrived
at Parawai. Their journey was ended, for they had
reached the dwelling place of his daughter, and of his
daughter-in-law, and of the two children, Uenuku and
Tama-ihu-toroa.

The following day Hinetekakara said to Kahu, "Sir,
Marupunganui has crossed over to the main land."

"Where ?" inquired Kahu.

"To the Ngae."

Then said Kahu, "To-morrow we will go to Motu-
tapu."

So when daylight came they set out, and found
Tu-o-rotorua dwelling on the island; but his father was
not there. Tu welcomed Kahu in these words:
"Come my *teina* to your island to be its *Ariki.*"

"Yes," replied Kahu, "this sacred island is mine;
but do you, my *Ariki*, continue to dwell on it."

Thus the island was given up to Tu-o-rotorua. But the *mana* of the land was Kahu's. Hence the song of Taipari before mentioned[1]; for Taipari sprang from the race of Tama-ihu-toroa. Tama's son was Tuara, and Tuara was an ancestor of Taipari.

As they paddled away from Motu-tapu Kahu bid farewell to Tu-o-rotorua—" Abide there, my child, you and your father. Alas! that I have not seen your father."

" Go, sir, go," were the parting words of Tu. " Go to guard your ancestor; go to the Arawa."

Leaving their canoes at the Toanga they went on towards Maketu. On the way Kahu's grandchild became thirsty, and cried for water. Kahu had compassion for the child, and chanted a *karakia*, and when the *karakia* was ended he stamped on the ground, and water came forth. Hence that place was named Te Wai-takahi-a-kahu (the water of Kahu's stamping).

Kahu afterwards remained at Maketu, and died, and was buried there. When he died the *mana* of Maketu went to his son Tawaki-moe-tahanga. When Tawaki died, the *mana-rahi* of Maketu went to Uenuku, who also died at Maketu when an old man. Then his son Rangitihi abandoned Maketu, and went to Rotorua, and settled at Matapara with all his family.

When Kahu left Ihenga at Kaipara at the dwelling place of his elder brother Taramainuku, he thus bid him farewell—" Sir, be quick to return to your child, my grandchild, Tama-ihu-toroa. Do not delay." So Ihenga remained at Kaipara for a short time. Then travelling

[1] P. 75.

northwards he came to Ripiro. The food of that place
was *toheroa*. Kupe placed it there for food for his
daughter, Tai-tu-auru-o-te-marowhara. The great rolling
waves on that coast have been named after her. So says
the proverb, " *Tai-hau-auru i whakaturia e Kupe ki te
Maro-whara*." Going on they arrived at a certain place
where Ihenga ate all their *toheroa* privately in the absence
of his companions.

" Who has eat our food ?" inquired his companions.

" How should I know ?" said Ihenga.

"Why, there was no one but you. You alone remained
here."

So they named the place Kai-hu-a-Ihenga. As they
were travelling they came to a hill. No water could be
found, and they were parched with thirst; so Ihenga
repeated a *karakia*, and then stamping on the ground a
spring of water flowed. Down flew pigeons in flocks to
drink the water. So the place was named Waikereru
(wood-pigeon water). Afterwards they came to a swamp
and a small river. A tree had fallen across the stream
by means of which they crossed. But the dog Potakatahiti was killed by the tree rolling on it. Then Ihenga
repeated a *karakia*, saying to the tree—" O tree lying
there, raise your head, raise your head."[1] And the tree
raised its head. Afterwards when he reached the higher
ground Ihenga saw a tree standing by itself in the centre
of the swamp. It was a *totara* tree. Then by the power
of his *karakia* he made a path for his dog that it might

---

[1] " *Te rakau e takoto nei, tungou, tungou* " are the *Maori* words.
Tungou = ἀνανεύω—a sign of dissent with the Greeks, but the
common sign of assent with the *Maori*.

go within the tree, and remain there for ever. And he said to the spirit of the dog, "If I cry '*moi, moi,*' you must answer 'au.' If I cry, '*ō, ō,*' you must answer '*ō, ō.*' If I say, 'Come, we two must go on,' you are to answer, 'Go, you, I cannot come.' If a party of travellers come this way hereafter, and rest on this hill, when you hear them speaking, you must speak to them. If the travellers say, 'Let us go,' you are to say 'Go.'" So the spirit of the dog was left to dwell within that tree; and ever since it mocks living men of the generations after Ihenga, even to our time.

At length Ihenga reached Mataewaka at the Kawakawa, where his elder brother Warenga dwelt. He remained there one month, and when the new moon appeared he and his brother Warenga went to the lake Te Tiringa to fish. There *inanga* were caught, some of which Ihenga preserved in a gourd filled with water, in order that he might carry them alive to Rotorua. He also caught some *koura*, or small cray fish, which he preserved alive in the same manner. This done, the brothers parted.

Ihenga travelled by way of Waiomio, giving names to places as he went. Te Ruapekapeka was named from the thousands of bats found there in the hollows of the trees. Also Tapuae-haruru, from the noise made by his footsteps. The sons of his brother Warenga were his companions. They made known the names given by Ihenga. Maiao was one of these sons. The son of Maiao was Te Kapotai, who was an ancestor of Tamati Waka Nene.

The hill Motatau was so called from Ihenga talking to himself. Going on they came to a river where Ihenga saw his own image in the still water, so the river was named Te Wai-whakaata-a-Ihenga (Ihenga's looking-glass). They came to another river, and dug up some worms to throw into the water. The fish would not come to the bait. Then Ihenga threw into the water some of his *inanga*. Then he called the eels, but they did not come. He called the *inanga*, and they came. He called the worms, and they came. Then he called on Tangaroa, and Tangaroa sent the eels. The mode of calling was a *karakia*. Going on he ascended a mountain. There he called on Thunder. He commenced his *karakia*, and as soon as it was finished thunder was sent, and lightning struck the top of the mountain, which is still named Whatitiri, or Thunder.

When they arrived at Whangarei they collected some muscles from a shoal, and roasted them on the fire, and that place is still called "Te Ahi-pupu-a-Ihenga"(Ihenga's muscle fire).

The chief of that place was Tahu-whakatiki, the eldest son of Hei. When the Arawa reached Wangaparoa Tahu and his younger brother Waitaha quarrelled. So Tahu and his family remained behind, while Waitaha and his father went on in the Arawa. Then Ihenga embarked in a canoe belonging to Te Whanau-a-Tahu. Two of the sons of Tahu—Te Whara and his younger brother Hikurangi- -went with him in the canoe. They touched at Taranga,[1] and sailing by Hauturu[2] they reached Moehau.

During one month Ihenga remained with his brother Huarere, and then went to Maketu. There he found his father-in-law, and his wife Hinetekakara, and his son

---

[1] The islands Hen and Chickens.   [2] The Little Barrier island.

Tama-ihu-toroa. So he remained a short time at Maketu, and then returned with his wife and son to Rotorua.

The *inanga* which he had brought with him from the Kawakawa he placed in the stream Waitepuia at Maketu. Before going to Rotorua he again caught them, and carried them with him in a gourd of water, and placed them in the lake ; but the *koura* he placed in the water at Parawai.

CHAPTER VII.

Sunt autem privata nullâ naturâ, sed aut vetere occupatione, ut qui quondam in vacua venerunt; aut victoriâ, ut qui bello potiti sunt; aut lege, pactione, conditione, sorte.—Cicero de Off., Lib. 1, ch. vii.

If you were to make inquiry from a New Zealander as to his land-title, it would be difficult to obtain from him reliable information as to any general rules of proceeding; for he would at once consider some particular case in which he was himself personally interested, and would give an answer corresponding with his interest therein. This may be due partly to the inaptitude of the Maori to take an abstract view of anything, which has been already noticed[1]. But it is doubtless from this cause that persons having competent knowledge of their language have expressed different opinions on this subject, founded on information thus obtained.

There are three reliable sources, however, from which such information can be obtained.

1. From *Maori* narratives, wherein matters relating to their land-titles are incidentally mentioned.

2. From Proverbs relating to the disposition of land among themselves.

3. From investigations of titles to land offered for sale, or when in dispute among themselves.

In the early days of the colony disputes about land

[1] p. 5

were of frequent occurrence, and the Government was often appealed to by one or other of the disputants.

From the foregoing *Maori* narrative[1] we learn that, after the canoe Arawa reached this island, the crew did not form a united and compact settlement at one place, as might have been expected. The names of nine chiefs are recorded who dispersed themselves north and south of the place where the canoe was dragged on shore, each going off in search of lands for himself and his own family.

Of these chiefs three went to Taupo, two to Wanganui, one to Rotorua, one to Mercury Bay, and one to Cape Colville; at the same time leaving behind at Maketu some members of their families. In the third generation two divisions of the family who had been settled about Cape Colville migrated, the one to the Bay of Islands, and the other to Kaipara.

From the narrative above referred to it also appears that the lands thus taken possession of were considered as rightfully belonging to the first occupier and his descendants, and that names were forthwith given to a great many places within the boundaries claimed, these names being frequently such as would make them sacred to the family, from being derived from names of persons or things to which some family sacredness was attached.

MANA.

The chief of any family who discovered and took possession of any unoccupied land obtained what was called the *mana* of the land. This word *mana*, in its ordinary use, signifies power, but in its application to

Vid. ch. v.

and corresponds somewhat with the power of a Trustee. Thus *mana* gave a power to appropriate the land among his own tribe according to a well recognized rule which was considered *tika* or straight. Such appropriation, however, once made, remained in force, and gave a good title to the children and descendants of the person to whom it had been thus appropriated. The *mana* of the acknowledged representative of the tribe had then only power over the lands remaining unappropriated, which power was more especially termed the *mana rahi* or great *mana*—the *mana* over appropriated land being with the head of the family in rightful possession. In course of time quarrels and wars arose between different tribes, so that tribes nearly allied to each other united for mutual defence and protection; and all the *Maori* of New Zealand came to be divided, for this purpose, into a few large tribes, each representing generally the crew of one of the various canoes composing the migration from Hawaiki. These being frequently at war with each other, it came to pass that every man who did not belong to a particular tribe was considered in respect to it as a *tangata ke* or stranger.

It has been affirmed by many on presumed good authority that no member of a tribe has an individual right in any portion of the land included within the boundaries of his tribe. Such, however, is not the case, for individuals do sometimes possess exclusive rights to land, though more generally members of families, more or less numerous, have rights in common to the exclusion of the rest of the tribe over those portions of land which have been appropriated to their ancestors. Their proverbs touching those who wrongfully remove boundary-marks show this, if other evidence were wanting.

The lands of a tribe, in respect to the title by which they are held, may be conveniently distinguished under two comprehensive divisions.

1. Those portions which have been appropriated, from time to time, to individuals and families.

2. The tribal land remaining unappropriated.

Whenever land is appropriated formally by native usage, it descends in the family of its first owners according to well recognized rules, and the *mana* of the representative of the tribe ceases to have any control over it. Their laws as to succession naturally tended to render the greater part of such lands the property of several of the same family as tenants in common; but an individual might and did frequently become a sole owner.

The tribal lands never specially appropriated belonged to all under the *mana*[1] or trusteeship of the tribal representative.

[1] Latterly a practice has been adopted of handing over the *mana* of their land to Matutaera, the Maori king, or to some influential chief in whom they have trust, the object being to protect it from clandestine sales, which have become frequent through the action of speculators in land. The agents who act for men of capital who enter into such speculations are always ready to offer an advance of money as a deposit on land, and when a *Maori*, especially a careless young man, visits our towns he is too often unable to resist the temptation of gold to be had for the mere signature of his name. When, however, such a transaction becomes known to the tribe it gives rise to much heart burning and trouble; but the thin end of the wedge being thus

Long before our colonists came to New Zealand land was of great value in *Maori* estimation, and was given and received as a suitable equivalent or compensation in certain cases.

Thus when a peace was concluded between two tribes land was sometimes given up as a sort of peace offering, but in a remarkably equitable spirit, it was always the tribe that had suffered least who, in such cases, gave some land to compensate the greater losses in war of the other party.

Such a mode of making peace seems to have been adopted in case of civil war between divisions of the same tribe, especially when waged with no prospect of either party completely mastering the other, and with the consideration of preventing both suffering such serious loss as would render them unable to cope with a common foe.

Also, in cases of adultery a piece of land would be demanded by the injured person; and his demand would be respected, for such was the proper compensation for the injury—land for the woman. But then a stratagem was sometimes employed, for when the injured man went to take profession, he might find his right opposed by some of the owners of the land who had purposely absented themselves from the conference whereat it was

introduced ere long others follow the example, till at length a sort of forced consent is obtained to pass the land, to use the common phrase, through the Government Land Court. It is therefore not to be wondered at that this Court is not in good repute among them, more especially since they have discovered that a large share of the purchase money is swallowed up by costs for survey, costs of the Court, and lawyers' fees.

given up.   And this unfair practice has sometimes been seized on as a precedent in their dealings with the *Pakeha*; for they have too often shown a readiness to sell lands to which they had only a joint right with many others, knowing well that those others would repudiate their act.

DESCENT OF LAND.

1. Male children succeed to their father's land, female children to their mother's land.

So says the proverb—"*Nga tamariki tane ka whai ki te ure tu, nga tamariki wahine ka whai ki te u-kai-po.*" "Male children follow after the male, female children follow after the breast fed on at night."

2. If a female marries a man of another tribe—*he tangata ke*—she forfeits all right to land in her mother's tribe.

So says the proverb—"*Haere atu te wahine, haere maro-kore.*" "The woman goes, and goes without her smock."

3. The children of a female married to a man of a stranger tribe have no right of succession to land in their mother's tribe."

So says the proverb—"*He iramutu tu ke mai i tarawahi awa*[1]"—"A nephew or niece standing apart on the other side of the river."

But there is a provision which can be applied to modify this last rule.   If the brothers of the woman ask for one or more of the children—their *iramutu*—to be given up to their care, and they are thus, as it were,

---

[1] This proverb was also applied in case of a war as a sufficient reason for not sparing such relation.

adopted by their uncles, they become reinstated in the tribal rights which their mother had forfeited.

A NEW ZEALANDER'S WILL.

Under this title in a former publication[1] I gave a literal translation of a written communication which I received from the celebrated Wi Tamihana Tarapipipi of Matamata, as follows :—

"A certain man had a male child born to him, then another male child, and then another male child. He also had daughters. At last the father of this family being at the point of death, the sons and daughters and all the relations assembled to hear his last words, and to see him die. And the sons said to their father: ' Let thy mouth speak, O father, that we may hear your will ; for you have not long to live.' Then the old man turned towards his younger brothers, and spoke thus :—

' Hereafter, O my brothers, be kind to my children. My cultivations are for my sons. Such and such a piece of land is for such and such a nephew. My eel-weirs, my potato gardens, my potatoes, my pigs, my male slaves, and my female slaves are for my sons only. My wives are for my younger brother.'

Such is the disposition of a man's property ; it relates only to his male children."

From this it appears that the head of a family had a recognized right to dispose of his property among his male offspring and kinsmen, and that his will expressed shortly before his death in the presence of his family

---

[1] Traditions and Superstitions of the New Zealanders.   Edit. 2, p. 271.

assembled for that purpose possessed all the solemnity
of a legal document.

RAHI.

is the term applied to a tribe reduced to a dependant
condition by a conquering tribe. The same authority
says, "Hear the custom in regard to lands which are
held by right of conquest, that is lands fallen to the
brave *(kua riro i te toa)*. Suppose some large tribe
is defeated. Suppose that tribe is defeated a second
and a third time, till at last the tribe becomes small, and
is reduced to a mean condition. It is then made to do
the work of dependants—to cultivate the land for food,
to catch eels, and to carry wood. In short, its men are
treated as slaves. In such a case their land passes into
the possession of the tribe whose valour conquered
them. They will not think of striving against their
masters; because their power to fight has gone from
them. They were not brave enough to hold possession
of their land, and although they may grow numerous
afterwards, they will not seek for a payment for their
former losses; for they are fearful, and say among themselves, 'Don't let us strive with this tribe, lest we perish
altogether, for it is a brave tribe.'"

William Thompson belonged to a victorious tribe:
his sentiments therefore have a natural bias in favour of
the sole right to the lands of the conquered tribe being
with their conquerors. If, however, a member of the
conquered tribe were to be consulted on this point, we
should learn that he had not abandoned all idea of a right
in the lands he had been allowed to retain, and was then
occupying. Instances could be referred to where the
conquered remnant of a tribe had regained power enough

to re-possess themselves of the lands formerly their own;
and in all cases where the conquerers have sold the
lands of their tributaries the latter have resisted the right
of the sellers to dispose thereof irrespectively of their
own interests therein.

NGATI-HANUI.

One day a chief named Hanui and his travelling
companion Heketewananga fell in with the old chief
Korako seated in the hollow trunk of a tree, which he
had converted into a temporary abode.   Then said
Hanui's companion, " I will make water on the old man's
head, to degrade him (lit., that his growth may be
stunted)." Hanui was displeased ; for the old man was
his cousin, being the son of the younger brother of his
father Maramatutahi , that was the cause of his displeasure at the words of his companion. But that fellow
Heketewananga persisted. He would not listen to the
anger of Hanui, but climbed the tree in order to make
water on the head of the old man. And when he had
done so, he jeered at the old man. " Ho ! ho ! now
then your growth is stunted because of my water; for
your head has been made water on."

With this Hanui and his companion went on their way.
When they were gone Korako also went to seek his son.
When he reached the bank of the river Waikato he saw
some boys on the other side of the river at play near their
Pa, and called to them, " Go and tell Wainganui to
bring a canoe for me." " We will bring a canoe," said
the boys. But the old man said " No. I don't wish
you to bring the canoe. Go and call Wainganui. He
himself must bring the canoe." So the boys went and
told Wainganui, " Your father is calling you to go to

him with a canoe." "Why did not you go?" said
Wainganui. "We offered to take the canoe to him,"
said the boys, "but he was not willing. He said that
you must take the canoe to him." So Wainganui went
in a canoe, and when he reached the other side of the
river he called to his father to come down to him.
But his father said, "Do you come up here to my side."
So Wainganui left the canoe and went to his father; for
he knew that he had something important to say to him.
Then seating himself by his father's side he said "What
means this that you have done?" The father said, "My
son, I have been wronged by your uncle Hanui and by
Heketewananga." "What sort of wrong?" inquired
the son. "My wrong," said the old man—"my wrong.
Heketewananga climbed on top of my house, and made
water on my head—at the same time he jeered me, ' Ho!
ho! now then your growth is stunted.'" Then the son
said to his father, "Ha! you were all but murdered by
those men. Their act shall be avenged. Their heads
shall soon be struck by my weapon." Then turning in
anger he went back to his canoe, and returned to the
Pa.

Without delay he called together the whole tribe, and
made known to them all that his father had told him.
After the tribe had heard the wrong done to their old
chief, they assembled at night to deliberate, and determined to go the next morning to kill those men. Then
they retired to rest. At daybreak they arose and armed
themselves, in number three hundred and forty, and set
out for the *Pa* at Hanui.

The men within that *Pa* were more than six hundred.
So when they saw the armed party coming to attack the

I

Pa, the six hundred rushed out to fight, and a battle took place outside. The men of the *Pa* were driven back, and the conquerors entered it with them. Then while the men of the *Pa* were being struck down Wainganui shouted to Hanui, " Be quick, Hanui, climb on top of your house, you and your children and your wives." So Hanui and his children and his wives climbed on the roof of their house. But most of the men of his tribe were killed, some only being left to be a *Rahi*, in which condition they now remain.

TAPUIKA.

It may happen that a tribe is driven off its lands by a conquering tribe, who may hold possession of the conquered lands for many years, but be, in their turn, driven off by the assistance of tribes allied to the original possessors of the land. It then becomes a question what right the allied tribes acquire in the recovered lands. A case of this sort came under my notice thus: I was instructed to purchase for the Government a piece of land of moderate size at Maketu to be occupied as a Mission station. As I had built a house on this land on a title of mere right of occupation, or as expressed in Maori, " *Noho noa iho*," and had resided there for some time, I thought, naturally, that the persons, at whose invitation my house had been placed there, were the persons to whom the land belonged. An arrangement was therefore made with them for the purchase of the land required, and a price agreed on. One night shortly after I was awoke from sleep by a knocking at the door of my house. My visitors were a deputation from some of the tribe Tapuika who had a small *Pa* below my house by the river side, at some distance from the large *Pa* by the mouth of the river. Their business was to warn me not to complete the purchase of the land, the persons with whom I had contracted being, as they affirmed, only occupiers and not owners thereof; whereas their tribe Tapuika were the owners, and the *mana* of the land belonged to their chief Te Koata. They came by night because they did not wish their interference to be known publicly, as it would cause disputes. And it did cause dispute when their nocturnal visit and its object was made public the next morning. However a good result came of it, for it was agreed that the question of title should be referred to the decision of the chiefs of the whole Arawa tribes.

A general assembly of the tribes consequently met at Rotorua, when it was shown that the land I proposed to purchase came within the old boundaries of Tapuika. But several generations before the present the *Pa* at Maketu had been taken by the hostile tribe Ngatiawa, and the Arawa tribes, including Tapuika, had been driven from the sea-coast to Rotorua and elsewhere. When the flax trade with Sydney was in vigour, many of the Arawa natives had been permitted to return to scrape flax for sale to a trader named Tapsell who was stationed at Maketu; and at length the combined Arawa tribes expelled Ngatiawa, and recovered the lands of their forefathers. They then established themselves in force at Maketu, and some of them marked out by boundaries, and took possession of land originally belonging to Tapuika, for their own use. Tapuika did not offer any objection to this, but now said that the land so taken was merely given up for their occupation, and that the *mana* of their chief Te Koata over the land had never been given up.

The decision of the chiefs of the Arawa, to which Te Koata, who was present, assented, was that as Tapuika could not have recovered their lands if unassisted by other Arawa tribes, the land of Tapuika which had been taken possession of by the fighting men of the combined tribes now belonged to those men, or expressed in their own words, " *kua riro i te toa,*" had gone to the brave.

This decision was important, as it established a precedent of value in dealing with any lands similarly circumstanced elsewhere in New Zealand—a precedent being always a powerful argument with the *Maori*.

THE EARLY SETTLERS.

When foreigners, called by the natives *Pakeha,* first came to New Zealand, they were admitted readily by the *Maori* to dwell among them. They were allowed to acquire land by purchase, and to form alliances with their families; and the children of such connections were considered as belonging to the tribe of their mother. They were never treated as belonging to a stranger tribe —as *tangata ke*. *Taku pakeha, toku matua,* my own *pakeha,* my father, were the common terms used to denote their sentiment of relationship.

It is not to be wondered at that every tribe in these islands was at first anxious to have *Pakeha* settlers dwelling with them, and was ready to admit them to the privileges of tribesmen, for through them they could obtain what they most valued of the world's goods.   But

when dissensions arose between the two races, notably
about land, and issued in war, the feelings of those who
took up arms became modified, and their old friends, the
Pakeha, were no longer looked on as *matua* or fathers,
but rather as *tangata ke*, or strangers.

THE WAITARA DISPUTE.

It is a recognised mode of action among the *Maori*, if
a chief has been treated with indignity by others of
his own tribe, and no ready means of redress can be
obtained, for the former to do some act which will
bring trouble on the whole tribe. This mode of obtaining
redress is termed "*whakahe*," and means putting the
other in the wrong. Strange to say, this very dangerous
principle of action, by whatever great evils it may be
followed, obtains the respect and not the censure of
the whole tribe for the person who adopts it.

Being in the neighbourhood of Matamata some years
ago, not long before the war broke out in Waikato, I
heard in conversation with a chief[1] of Ngatihaua, who
had taken part in the war at Taranaki, that the reason
why Teira proposed to sell Waitara was to obtain
satisfaction for a slight put upon him by Wi Kingi in
connection with a private quarrel.[2] I never had an
opportunity to verify the facts narrated, but there was in
them nothing improbable, and according to *Maori* usage
they accounted for Teira having acted as he did.

The land thus offered for sale was estimated to contain
about six hundred acres, the whole of which had, in

---

[1] Paora Te Ahuru.
[2] "*Hei whakahe mo Wiremu Kingi*" was the expression used.

former years, been thickly inhabited, and apportioned among a great many individuals and families. It was therefore of the character comprised under our division No. 1. Teira and those more nearly allied to him offered to sell the whole six hundred acres, in opposition to the wish of Wi Kingi and others who claimed rights in the land.

That Kingi and his party had substantial claims to portions of this land, and that such was the original ground of his opposition to the sale appears from several letters written by natives at the time as a kind of protest, particularly from one written by Riwai Te Ahu in which he says: "The reason why Wiremu Kingi and his party made so much objection, when Teira proposed that the place should be sold to the Governor, was the fear lest their land and ours should be all taken as belonging to Teira."

A chief of great influence well supported has no doubt frequently acted as if he could dispose of large tracts of land without consulting others who had rights included therein. But he never thought of asserting a right to ignore *in toto* the rights of others not parties to the sale. On the contrary, the chief and they who had shared the purchase money would say to other claimants who had not received any part of the payment, either that they should be satisfied out of a future payment (for it was a general, though an impolitic and bad custom, to pay by instalments in such transactions), or that they might themselves apply to the purchaser for payment of their interests, or that they might hold fast to their own.

If before paying any part of the purchase money to

Teira, he had been required to mark out the boundaries of those portions of the six hundred acres which he and his party claimed, the *onus probandi* would have been placed on the right man. It would then have been discovered that those portions were detached and of various shapes and sizes, and in some cases only to be approached by narrow paths, and that some of his boundaries were disputed. For all which reasons what he could have rightfully sold would have been of little value for the occupation of our colonists.

But in addition to any claim of Wi Kingi and others whom he represented to the ownership of portions of the six hundred acres offered for sale by Teira, they had a further right not to be disturbed in their holdings, which does not appear to have been considered at the time.

When the Te Ati-awa tribes determined to abandon Cook's Straits and return to the lands of their ancestors about Taranaki, they were still in dread of their old enemies the Ngatimaniapoto. It was therefore arranged among them, for their better security, that they should form one united settlement on the south bank of the Waitara—thus placing the river between themselves and the common enemy. Supposing, therefore, that Wi Kingi and his division of the tribe had no land actually their own by ancient right at the place thus occupied, they had acquired a right by virtue of the arrangement made, a right recognised by old native custom, on the faith of which they had expended their labour in building houses, as well as in fencing and cultivating the land, to disturb which, in a summary manner, could only be looked on as an offensive act. We have seen also how

in relation to the dispute between Tapuika and the
Arawa tribes it was adjudged by general consent that
the latter had acquired a permanent right to the lands
which they had occupied under somewhat similar circumstances.

There appears little reason to doubt that Teira's pro-
posal to sell Waitara was prompted by a vindictive
feeling towards Wi Kingi; for he knew well that by
such mode of proceeding he would embroil those who
would not consent with their European neighbours. At
the same time it is a rather mortifying reflection that
the astute policy of a *Maori* chief should have prevailed
to drag the Colony and Her Majesty's Government into
a long and expensive war to avenge his own private
quarrel.

APPENDIX.

MAORI TERMS OF RELATIONSHIP.

TUPUNA. *An ancestor—male or female.*

MATUA. *A father, or uncle either patruus or avunculus.*

PAPA. *The same.*

WHAEA. *A mother, or aunt on either side.*

TAMA. *Eldest nephew.*

TAMAHINE. *Eldest niece; also used more generally.*

TAMAITI. *Son, or nephew.*

TAMAROA. *The same.*

TUAKANA. *Elder brother of males, elder sister of females; also elder brother's children in reference to younger brother's children, elder sister's children in reference to younger sister's children.*

TEINA. *The younger brother of males, the younger sister of females; also the younger brother's children in reference to elder brother's children, the younger sister's children in reference to elder sister's children.*

TUNGANE. *A sister's brother.*

TUAHINE. *A brother's sister.*

IRAMUTU. *A nephew, or niece.*

HUNGAWAI. *A father-in-law, or mother-in-law.*

HUNAONGA. *A son-in-law, or daughter-in-law.*

TAOKETE. *A man's brother-in-law, or sister's sister-in-law.*

AUTANE. *A woman's brother-in-law.*

AUWAHINE. *A man's sister-in-law.*

POTIKI. *A brother's children, or sister's children; also the youngest child of a family.*

MOKOPUNA. *A grand-child, or child of a nephew or niece.*

HUANGA. *A relation in general.*

WHANAUNGA-TUPU. *A blood relation.*

ARIKI. *The first born male or female.*

WAEWAE. *A man's younger brother: literally the foot.*

HAMUA. *Syn. tuakana.*

MARONUI. *A married man or woman.*

TAKAKAU. *A single man or woman.*

POUARU. *A widow.*

PUHI. *A betrothed female, also a female of rank restricted from marriage.*

HE WAHINE TAUMARO. *A betrothed female.* N.B.—There is a distinction between a *Puhi* and a *wahine taumaro.* The betrothed female is a *Puhi* in reference to her father's act of consent, and a *wahine taumaro* in reference to her future father-in-law's act of consent to the arrangement.

VOCABULARY

OF SOME MAORI WORDS REQUIRING EXPLANATION.

IHI has the sense of *tapu* when occurring in *karakia*, or invocations of spirits.

KAHUKAHU, the spirit of the germ of a human being: also called *Atua noho-whare*, or house-dwelling *Atua.* Verbi *kahukahu* significatio simplex est panniculus; et panniculus quo utitur femina menstrualis nomine *kahukahu* dicitur κατ᾽ ἐξοχὴν. Apud populum Novæ Zelandæ creditur sanguinem utero sub tempus menstruale effusum continere germina hominis; et secundùm præcepta veteris superstitionis panniculus sanguine menstruali imbutus habebatur sacer *(tapu)*, haud aliter quàm si formam humanam accepisset: mulierum autem mos est hos panniculos intra juncos parietum abdere; et hâc de causâ paries est domûs pars adeo sacra ut nemo illi innixus sedere audeat.

KARAKIA. This word generally rendered by 'charm,' does not signify what the word charm would mean, in its popular sense. The word 'invocation' conveys more correctly its meaning; for it is a prayer addressed to spirits of deceased ancestors, in form somewhat like a litany.

KAUPAPA, one whom the spirit of an ancestor visits, and who is its medium of communication with the living.

PUKENGA, a spirit, the author or first teacher of any *karakia*.

TAPAIRU, any very sacred ancestral Spirit: also sometimes applied to the female *Ariki*.

TAUIRA, a person who is being instructed by a *tohunga*, or by the spirit of a parent or ancestor. He had to submit to a strict fast of several days before he was taught any important *karakia*.

TIPUA, or TUPUA, the spirit of one who when living was noted for powerful *karakia*.

TIRI, a strip of flax leaf or *toetoe* so placed as to serve as an imaginary pathway for an *Atua*. In sickness a *tiri* is suspended above the head of the sick person to facilitate the departure of the *Atua* who causes the disease. A *tiri* is also suspended near the *kaupapa*, when he desires his *Atua* to visit him. It is also applied to signify the *karakia* used on such occasions.

TOHUNGA, a person skilled in *karakia*, also one skilled in any craft.

Tuahu, a sacred place where offerings of food—first fruits—for the *Atua* were deposited.

Wananga, the spirit of anyone who when living had learned the *karakia* of his ancestors: thus when a *tauira* died he became a *wananga*.

TE KARAKIA

Mo te pikinga o Tawhaki ki te Rangi.—*vid.* p. 23.

Piki ake Tawhaki i te ara kuiti
I whakatauria ai te ara o Rangi,
Te ara o Tu-kaiteuru.
Ka kakea te ara wha-iti,
Ka kakea te ara wha-rahi,
Ko te ara i whakatauria ai
To tupuna a Te Ao-nunui,
A Te Ao-roroa,
A Te Ao-whititera.
Tena ka eke
Kei to Ihi,
Kei to Mana,
Kei nga mano o runga,
Kei o Ariki,
Kei o Tapairu,
Kei o Pukenga,
Kei o Wananga,
Kei o Tauira.

TE TUKU O HINE-TE-IWAIWA.—*vid.* p. 28.

Raranga, raranga tăku takapau,
Ka pukea e te wai,
Hei moenga mo aku rei.
Ko Rupe, ko Manumea,
Ka pukea: ē! ē!
Mo aku rei tokorua ka pukea.
Ka pukea au e te wai,
Ka pukea, ē! ē!

Ko koro taku tane ka pukea.
Piki ake hoki au ki runga nei:
Te Matitikura, ē! ē!
Ki a Toroa irunga,
Te Matitikura, ē! ē!
Kia whakawhanaua aku tama
Ko au anake ra.
Tu te turuturu no Hine-rauwharangi;
Tu te turuturu no Hine-te-iwaiwa.
Tu i tou tia me ko Ihuwareware;
Tu i tou kona me ko Ihuatamai.
Kaua rangia au e Rupe.
Kei tauatia, ko au te inati,
Ko Hine-te-iwaiwa.
Tuku iho irunga i tou huru,
I tou upoko,
I ou tara-pakihiwi,
I tou uma,
I to ate,
I ou turipona,
I ou waewae.
E tuku ra ki waho.
Tuku ewe,
Tuku take,
Tuku parapara.
Naumai ki waho.

KARAKIA

Mo te wahine i pākia nga u i te whanautanga o te
tamaiti.—*vid.* p. 39.

Nga puna irunga te homai,
Te ringia ki te matamata
O nga u o tenei wahine;
Te kopata i te rangi te homai
Hei whakato mo nga u
O tenei wahine:
Ki te matamata o nga u

O tenei wahine:
Nga u atarere reremai
Ki te matamata o nga u
O tenei wahine:
Nga u atarere tukua mai.
Tenei hoki te tamaiti te tangi nei,
Te aue nei i te po nui,
I te po roa.
Ko Tu-te-awhiawhi,
Ko Tu-te-pupuke,
Naumai ki ahau,
Ki tenei tauira.

KARAKIA

Mo te whakapikinga o te ara o te tupapaku ana ka
mate, kia tika ai te haere ki nga mea kua mate atu
imua.—*vid.* p. 44.

Tena te ara, ko te ara o Tawhaki,
I piki ai ki te rangi,
I kake ai ki tou tini,
Ki tou mano:
I whano ai koe,
I taemai ai to wairua ora
Ki tou kaupapa.
Tenei hoki ahau
Te mihi atu nei,
Te tangi atu nei
Ki to wairua mate.
Puta purehurehu mai
To putanga mai ki ahau,
Ki to kaupapa,
I piri mai ai koe,
I tangi mai ai koe.
Tena te tiri,
Ko te tiri a o tupuna,
Ko te tiri a nga Pukenga,
A nga Wananga,
Aku, a tenei tauira.

HE WHAKAMURI-AROHA.—*vid.* p. 47-8.

Aha te hau e maene ki to kiri ?
E kore pea koe e ingo mai ki to hoa,
I piri ai korua i to korua moenga,
I awhi ai korua,
I tangi ai korua.
Tena taku aroha
Ma te hau e kawe ki a koe,
Huri mai to aroha,
Tangi mai ki to moenga,
I moe ai korua.
Kia pupuke—a—wai to aroha.

TE POROPORO-AKI A TAMA-TE-KAPUA.—*vid.* p. 53.

E papa nga rakau i runga i a koe,
Mau ake te Whakāro ake. Ae, Ae.
E haere nga taua i te ao nei,
Mau e patu. Ae, Ae.